MW00628418

Ed Tandy McGlasson

How to
BECOME
the Husband and Father Your Family Needs

ENDORSEMENTS

"Ed, this is the book I wish I'd had to read one day before my son was born."

Bobb Biehl
Executive Mentor, Scottsdale, Arizona

"So many men believe the key to becoming strong and godly husbands and fathers is to work harder and do more. But in this inspiring new book, Ed Tandy McGlasson encourages us first to humbly receive what Christ has given us. From there, our most important relationships can thrive as we live out of the love and blessings God has bestowed so freely upon us."

Jim Daly
President, Focus on the Family

"There are few jobs more important than being a father. But so many dads feel unequipped and a bit overwhelmed by the responsibility. Ed Tandy McGlasson provides a deeply personal, practical and biblical approach to the task. In a warm and vulnerable voice, he guides all fathers to the principles and tools that will help. Highly recommended."

John Townsend, Ph.D.
Author of the *New York Times* bestselling *Boun•aries* series
Founder, the Townsend Institute for Leadership and Counseling

"Many men today struggle as fathers because they weren't fathered right themselves. Ed gives great tools and encouragement to men who are desperately seeking to raise godly children and build marriages of respect and love. Ed is candid about both his struggles and his victories and his stories will inspire you to be the man God wants you to be."

Ken Harrison
President and chairman of Promise Keepers
CEO of WaterStone, a Christian Community Foundation

"If you've ever longed for a heart coach to walk alongside you to find healing for your deepest longings from a Father, this book is for you. Though written primarily to men, this is a fantastic book for any woman who is ready to receive more from God as her Father. Ed Tandy McGlasson leads us to be open and authentic alongside him as he weaves heart-warming stories of struggle and resilience with biblical truths and practical how-to's as we're personally invited to embrace being fathered by God."

Dr. Michelle Watson

Author of *Let's Talk: Conversation Starters for Da∙s an∙ Daughters*
and radio/podcast host of *The Da∙ Whisperer*

"Ed McGlasson and I first met in 1981 when we both played for the Los Angeles Rams. Two years later we became brother-in-laws. I've had a front-row seat watching Ed live out the chapters of the book you now hold in your hands. I know he will lead you on a journey to becoming a better father and husband!"

George Andrews

1979-1985 Los Angeles Rams, husband, father, mentor

"In the NFL, you could always tell the ballplayers who were raised without the blessing of the father. They were weak, they complained, they were easily distracted, they lashed out, they were empty shells. When a son or daughter has been blessed by the father, they are strong, capable, they grow, they learn, they help and they serve. God gave us an example. Thanks, Ed for taking this most courageous journey on in your ministry. This book is a game plan for every father who wants to make a difference. It's important and urgent!"

Brian Holloway

New England Patriots All-Pro
Stanford, Harvard, Wharton, www.Brianholloway.com

"Thanks, Ed, for this powerful, personal and transformative book. My dad, Jack Kemp, was an awesome, bigger-than-life father, who loved, encouraged and blessed me. But still, my identity wasn't complete until I received the blessing of the perfect Father. Being His son makes me the husband and father my family needs. This book opened my heart to more of God the Father's extravagant and generous heart. Every man needs this to become the real and good man God made him to be. If you want to become that man, husband and father, this is your playbook."

Jeff Kemp
Former 11-year NFL Quarterback, Author of *Facing the Blitz*
Ambassador, speaker and coach for fatherhood, manhood and marriage at
www.JeffKempTeam.com

"Ed goes straight to the heart's desire of every man who wants to be an excellent husband and father. He combines great passion and practical biblical insight while helping men work on their inner healing. Ed is refreshingly filled with grace and is a great motivator to help us be a part of our greatest calling for our families."

Jim Burns, PhD
President, HomeWord
Author of *Doing Life with Your Adult Children: Keep Your Mouth Shut and the Welcome Mat Out*

"The Bible is known to be the best-selling book of all time, rightly so... I would impress upon you that *How to Become the Husband and Father Your Family Needs*, is right under that best-selling book! Without question, every father, son, brother, grandfather, man should read this book!! The message is profound, deeply touching and one of the most penetrating and important books of our time. The unparalleled message of the Father's blessing is one that cannot be silenced; our lives depend on it. If you love the men in your life, you will put this book in their hands."

Debbie Rasa
Owner/Partner of Rasa Floors

Copyright © 2020 Ed Tandy McGlasson
Published by Blessing of the Father Ministries
17602 17th St. Suite 102 #322
Tustin, California 92780
Printed in the United States of America by Printopya

All rights reserved. No part of this book may be reproduced in any form without the permission in writing from Blessing of the Father Ministries.

All scripture quotations, unless otherwise indicated, are from The Holy Bible, English Standard Version®, copyright © 2001 by Crossway, a publishing ministry of Good News Publishers. Used by permission. All rights reserved.

Scripture quotations marked MSG are taken from THE MESSAGE, copyright © 1993, 2002, 2018 by Eugene H. Peterson. Used by permission of NavPress Publishing Group. All rights reserved.

Scripture quotations marked NLT are taken from The Holy Bible, New Living Translation. Copyright © 1993, 2002, 2018. Used by permission of Tyndale House Publishers, a Division of Tyndale House Ministries. All rights reserved.

Scripture quotations labeled NIV are from the Holy Bible, New International Version®. NIV®. Copyright © 1973, 1978, 1984, 2011 by Biblica, Inc. Used by permission of Zondervan. All rights reserved worldwide. www.zondervan.com

Scripture quotations taken from the New American Standard Bible® (NASB), Copyright © 1960, 1962, 1963, 1968, 1971, 1972, 1973, 1975, 1977, 1995 by The Lockman Foundation Used by permission. www.Lockman.org

Scriptures marked TLB are taken from THE LIVING BIBLE (TLB): Scripture taken from THE LIVING BIBLE copyright© 1971. Used by permission of Tyndale House Publishers, Inc., Carol Stream, Illinois 60188. All rights reserved.

Cover design by my amazing sons: Edward and Josh Tandy McGlasson
Cover Photo by Duke Loren Photography

ISBN: 978-1-7350995-3-8
eISBN: 978-1-7350995-2-1

www.blessingofthefather.org

DEDICATION

To my beloved wife, Jill, the great love of my life—you have taught me how to love and have fun. I love doing life, love and family with you.

To my precious children: Edward and his wife, Kate; Jessica and her husband, Greg; Mary and her husband, Tim; Lukas and his wife, McKenna; and Joshua—you have given me my highest honor of being your father. You have prayed and taught me how to be a present father. I love watching you as you father and mother my amazing grandchildren: Isla Jeanne, Madeleine Grace, Gwendolin Angelika, Rauly Jordan, Anna Lee, and Colette Marie!

TABLE OF CONTENTS

ACKNOWLEDGMENTS

I first want to thank my beloved wife of over 37 years, Jill, who has loved me and called me her pastor since our first weeks together. You still take my breath away. You are my treasure, *mein Schatz*. Thank you for following this wild, passionate man, and teaching me what a present, loving father truly looks like. I couldn't have done it without you.

I want to thank Mary Pero for her compassion for and patience with me in writing and editing this book. You wouldn't be reading these pages without her hard work and gift of being a great writer. She has been my faithful assistant for the last five years and carries the heart of the Father wherever she goes. Mary and her amazing husband, Mark, have adopted three brothers and have given them a new beginning so they can connect to the love of the Father in their own story. You teach me every day what the Father's love in Christ looks like!

I want to thank Jeff Katke for his gift of writing with clarity. His wisdom and great questions have helped us focus our writing so we can clearly communicate to you, the reader. We are committed to helping you become the husband and father your family needs.

To Brian Holloway, who has been my best friend since high school and whose friendship has made me a better man, husband, and father. He has the ability to help maximize the gifts that God has given us. Thank you for being my friend.

To my men's group in Newport Beach that has met every Thursday morning for the last ten years: Jimmy, Dac, Wayne, Jeff, Paul, Lowell, Eddie, Doug, Stuart, Al, and John, who have walked with me, supported me in prayer, and taught me every week what a godly man looks like.

FOREWORD
by Brian Holloway

You are holding an amazing gift in your hands, *How to Become the Husband and Father Your Family Needs.* I have watched God the Father work this message into Ed's life and family. I have known Ed for the last 45 years and witnessed his transformation into becoming a great husband and father. He was raised the same way I was, we both had career military dads, and we met one another at Churchill High School football field in Potomac, Maryland. I saw this man running wind sprints and walked over and said, "Hey, you want to work out together?" He smiled and said, "Lets race."

We ran our first 50-yard sprint as Ed beat me by a step. I quickly said, "You are the first white boy to ever beat me in a race." He smiled and said, "Let's go again." We turned around and ran another sprint, and this time I beat Ed by a step. He said, "Well, you're the first black man to ever beat me." I knew at that moment I had found a friend who would push me to become the best I could be. We literally spent almost every waking moment that summer hanging out, clearing out my mom's refrigerator, much to my dad's chagrin.

We had a relationship that King David's son Solomon wrote about: "Iron sharpens iron, and one man sharpens another" (Prov. 27:17 ESV). That is what great friends do. Something powerful and profound happened to both of us that summer. Looking back, I know God put us together, because two are better than one, and both of us still carried a wound from our fathers that God would heal.

We trained together with NFL dreams, went through surgeries, and rehab together. We have worshiped, prayed, lifted one another up, spoken the truth, and lived out our stories that no one would ever imagine. I was with Ed when God started calling him out of the National Football League to follow Jesus and become a fisher of men. I don't think I have ever been around Ed where he didn't find someone around us to share Jesus with.

He has been an all-in man for Jesus since those first moments during a high school race, yes, like Brian's Song: to our journey as competitors, to the National Football League, New York Jets, New England Patriots, Philadelphia Eagles, New York Giants to the biggest stadium of all—becoming fathers!

Beyond the stadium of cheering fans, we both ran full speed into fatherhood with wonderful excitement and energy—only to discover a much more impor tant calling that required the heart and blessing of God the Father. My 8 children can testify, and Ed's 5 children can too. Something happened to Dad when he encountered Jesus and the blessing of the Father.

God has called us to make a difference as fathers, during a time when fathers are in short supply. This book will give you hope—and the courage you need to receive your true birthright as a beloved son of God so you can become the man you never thought you could be. It happened for me, and I am so grateful to have a playbook like this book to become the father my kids need me to be.

Maybe you're reaching up, or silently reaching out. This is a perfect read during what seems like the most uncertain of times. When you will feel the Father's loving embrace and blessing, your heart will heal; mine did. His loving hands will comfort your heart, restore your joy, and turn your story from your wounds to the laughter that comes back when we discover that God the Father loves us.

"… I will be a father to you, and you shall be sons and daughters to me, says the Lord Almighty" (2 Cor. 6:18 ESV).

This is one of the most important conversations a man needs to have with himself—as he reaches out to God as his Father and connects with Him.

Ed has reached men's hearts all over the world, from NFL Professional Athletes Outreach to Fellowship of Christian Athletes, and many more. And he will reach yours too.

Before I go, here's a secret:

When your wife, daughters, and sons see you reading this book–something powerful is happening. First, they will see that you want to be a better father. Second, they will watch the Holy Spirit move you and shape you into the husband and father your family needs.

Warning! Once you touch this rather ordinary, simple-looking book, the Holy Spirit will rise up in you—to become the man God has chosen to lead your family. You will hear the voice of the One who made the heavens and earth say to you, "Come and follow me, and I will make you into the husband and father your family needs."

It has been my pleasure to introduce you to my very best friend.

Brian Holloway
New England Patriots All-Pro
Stanford, Harvard, Wharton, www.Brianholloway.com,
Corporate Coach - Hired by 487 Fortune 500,
America's #1 Most Requested Teambuilder,
Digital Footprint 126,000,000 in 185 Countries

Introduction

A re you ready?" Dr. Medders said, as he joined my wife, Jill, and me in our hospital labor and delivery room. He was our OB/GYN doctor. Jill had been in labor for the past 18 hours and she was ready to push this baby out.

He looked at me with a smile and said, "Ed, you are about to become a father." He reached out his hand and grabbed mine; his hands were huge, perfectly designed to catch newborn babies. He said, "Your baby is ready to come. Do you want to deliver your son?"

"Me?" I asked.

He said, "Yes!"

I had recruited my dear mother-in-love, Nancy, to do the nurturing and handholding. I was trying to give Jill my best pregame locker-room football speech. She rolled her eyes as if she was saying, "Oh boy, here he goes again."

Our nurse helped me put on the blue hospital garment and the surgical gloves. Dr. Medders said, "Ed, he's coming. Get in there!"

I sat on a rolling stool to move into the place where the doctor usually sat. I remember the sound of the wheels rolling on the floor and the smell of the Betadine disinfectant still in the air.

I will never forget my wife's last push, as she transferred her first son, who we named Edward, into my hands as I caught him. He was slippery and beautiful at the same time. I had just become a father! I held Edward up, like Mustafa holding Simba, his firstborn, in *The Lion King*, with tears in my eyes, dedicating him to the Lord.

The doctor grabbed him, looked him over, and said, "Ten toes, ten fingers, he looks perfect." The nurse swaddled him in a blue baby blanket and handed him to Jill. We were both filled with a joy that was bigger than words could say. I was just given one of God's greatest gifts and callings. I was becoming a father.

The doctor's invitation to "get in there" was not only for me; it's also for every man who loves a woman and makes a baby. If you are a husband and a father, you are the perfect man to get in there and make a difference. There is no one who can replace you, no matter how you started your family. You might not have been able to be there for the birth of your children, but it is never too late for you to get in there to make a difference.

I wrote this book to give men hope that, in Christ, we can become the husband and father our families need. I might have been there at the birth of all my children, but I struggled with becoming a good father after they were born. My biological father died a military hero before I was born, and my stepfather, also in the military, traveled most of my childhood serving our country. He knew how to push me to overcome my fears but struggled to understand how to be a present father. I have always known that he loved me, but like many dads, he pushed me toward my dreams without knowing how to build a healthy relationship with me. My stepfather struggled to be a dad because his father didn't know how to be a good father to him.

I meet men like me every day who want to become good husbands and fathers but have never been shown how to do it. I will share with you some of those secrets I have learned from the life of Jesus that have transformed my relationship with my wife and children, and they will transform your life too.

I have witnessed tens of thousands of men encounter Jesus for themselves and receive the love and blessing of God the Father. When a man is fathered by God, the same way Jesus was, he understands who God has made him to be and how he can become the man, husband, and father his family needs.

We live in a world where Satan wants to destroy men and their God-given roles so that he can unravel their families and destroy their children. God made men to be the foundation of blessing for their families. If you want to destroy a marriage and a child, get rid of that husband and father.

But God has a plan! He promises,

> "Behold, I will send you Elijah the prophet before the great and awesome day of the LORD comes. And he will turn the hearts of fathers to their children and the hearts of children to their fathers, lest I come and strike the land with a decree of utter destruction." (Mal. 4:5–6)

Families will heal when a father's heart is turned back toward his children. I have met men all over the world who have built their careers but lost their children. I believe God is turning the hearts of fathers to their children. You are reading this book because you want to become the best husband and father you can be!

I wrote this book to help you understand the process of how to become the husband and father your family needs. Here's the good news: the same God who formed you in your mother's womb and knew you before you were born has called you to be an incredible man, husband, and father. You can do it because God has called you to do it. You can do it because God will give you everything you need to do it. You can do it because the Holy Spirit will empower you to do it. It doesn't matter where you've been or what you've done; it's never too late to become the husband and father your family needs.

Fortunately for me and my family, through an amazing encounter with Jesus, I discovered that God wanted to be my Father. God has made us to be fathered and blessed by Him. The blessing from God, the Father, started healing the man I was so that I could become the husband and father my family needed me to be. The Father's love changed my life forever. If He can transform a broken-down ex-professional football player into a good husband and father, then He can do it for you too.

This book is a collection of the best practices I have learned over thirty years of relationship with God the Father, through His Son, Jesus, regarding how to become the husband and father a family needs.

Are you ready to become the husband and father your family needs?

Get in there!

CHAPTER 1

The Receiving Principle

Truly, truly, I say to you, the Son can do nothing of his own accord, but only what he sees the Father doing. For whatever the Father does, that the Son does likewise.

John 5:19

I like to call allowing oneself to be fathered by God the Receiving Principle. It's the secret to being a great man, husband, and father. Our ability to be the father and husband our family needs depends upon our willingness to receive the blessing of the Father through Jesus Christ. When we receive the blessing of the Father into our hearts and minds and allow God to father us the way He fathered His Son, Jesus, our cup will be full. We can pour into our wife and children the same love and forgiveness the Father has poured into us. This is the Receiving Principle. We can't earn it; we just have to receive God's love and mercy. The Receiving Principle is all about following what the Father is doing the way Jesus did. When we are receiving like Jesus did, we don't take the lead on our own. Rather, we are always looking for what the Father is doing so that we can do likewise.

Are You Afraid of the Ball Now?

When I was ten years old, my stepdad took me to the baseball field to give me some coaching advice. It was mid-season and I had been in a hitting slump because I was afraid of being hit by the ball. Every time the pitcher threw the ball, I'd jump backward out of the batter's box as if the ball were hot on the inside of the plate. That day, the field was empty except for my stepfather and me. He placed a football helmet on my head and had me stand in the batter's box. I did not understand what was going on. I thought maybe we would do a little batting practice as Dad walked away toward the pitcher's mound. But that didn't really explain the football helmet.

Suddenly, and without warning, he began pelting me with fast balls one right after the other. They were coming at me so fast I could hardly swing the bat. WHACK! The first ball ricocheted off my helmet. THUD. A ball hit me in the leg. I was getting more and more upset with each pitch. WHOOSH! BAM! A ball rushed by my head and hit the backboard behind me. I finally pulled myself together and swung the bat. CRACK! The ball went flying, and thankfully my stepdad stopped pitching.

I was furious and crying as he walked up to me at the batter's box. "Are you afraid of the ball now? You've got nothing to be afraid of! No one in Little League will ever throw the ball as hard as I just did."

Dad solved a problem for me that day. I was never again afraid of being hit by the ball. I laugh when I think about that story now. My dad really was trying to help me! And like most sons, I wanted to please him. Unfortunately, his methods of teaching me to overcome my fears didn't do a lot for our relationship. I was angry and hurt by his methods but I stopped fearing being hit by a pitch.

The first lesson I learned was, don't be afraid of being hit by a ball. But the second lesson had a deeper effect on my relationship with Dad, my stepfather, and on my relationship with my children. The second lesson was one my dad didn't realize he was teaching me. That lesson was, to get his love and approval

I must perform to his standards. I cannot be afraid if I want my dad to love and approve of me. Or, he doesn't love me just because I'm his son; I need to perform well to get my dad's love and approval. That was not what he was trying to teach me.

As I grew older and heard more stories of his relationship with his own dad, I understood; he was doing the best he could with what he received from his father.

I remember one story he told me about how his father had helped him to overcome his fear of water. He was about thirteen years old when his dad took him out for a drive. He stopped on a bridge that went right over the river, pulled my dad out of the car, and threw him into the water! As he was struggling in the river, his father yelled, "Sink or swim! Die or try! It's up to you, boy, if you make it!" He suffered from his dad's brutal teaching method. His father unintentionally wounded him.

I can't tell you how many times I've told myself I would not repeat the same broken parenting patterns that my stepdad used with me. I wanted to be different. I wanted to be better. I wanted more for my kids. But guess what? As I look back over 37 years of raising my five children and all the good times we experienced, there were also moments when I fell short of being the father I wanted to be. Maybe you have too. I tried to be a good dad, yet there were times I could see where I still repeated the same broken patterns of my dad, just as he repeated the same broken patterns of his father.

Bear Country

Let me tell you about one of my low moments as a father that is also humorous. My son Edward came to me during one of our fishing trips and told me it scared him to go fishing because there were bears in the area. So I tried to do for Edward what my dad had done for me, to help him face his fear. I bravely told him, "Let's go fishing in bear country. Don't be afraid. Face your fears, son! If we run into a bear, then whatever you do, don't run away. You've got to stand your ground, show no fear, and stare him down."

We grabbed our fishing poles and headed up to a stream above Twin Lakes in the Sierra mountains, which is one of my favorite fishing streams (where I had never seen a bear before).

I was telling him, as we were walking, how to face a bear and not be afraid. We rounded a corner, and to my great surprise, a big black bear stood on his hind legs and roared at both of us. I looked at my son and said, "Run, or he will eat you!" In a few seconds, we were both running faster than we had ever run in our life back to our cabin. We stepped inside the cabin huffing and puffing. My wife, Jill, looked at Edward and me and asked, "What happened?" Edward said, "We almost got eaten by a bear, and Dad made me run rather than stand and stare the bear down." So much for teaching my son bravery. This is not one of my favorite moments. It was embarrassing but also hysterical.

Even though I promised myself that I would not throw baseballs at my sons' heads or throw my children in a river to help them overcome their fears, I almost got my son eaten by a bear by attempting to teach my boy a lesson in the same way my father did. While it is a funny story, the more I thought about it and how afraid Edward must have been, my head dropped, as I had missed the mark because I was repeating broken methods I had learned from my dad.

How many of you have sworn you would not hurt your kids the way you were hurt? Why do we do that? How do we break the cycle? In theory, it sounds great to say, "I will never treat my kids that way," and you may experience some victories; but overall, this plan doesn't work. Why? Because saying you won't do something doesn't give you the power or the ability to replace that negative practice with a better one. Like father, like son. We all repeat some of our learned behaviors from our parents. Some good. Some bad.

There's an old saying that goes, "You can't pour from an empty cup." It makes sense, doesn't it? If there's nothing in your cup, nothing will come out when you try to pour it into another cup. Let me give you an example. I spent years believing that if I just kept on trying to be that perfect dad, then eventually I would be.

But it didn't happen that way. As much as I tried, I kept repeating those same broken parenting patterns. I had to pour out into my kids. My cup was nearly empty because my dad's cup was empty, too.

Good Father, Good Son

Some of you have more in your cup to be a good father and husband. You received something from your father because he was present in your life. Fathering isn't about being perfect; so much of it is about being present. No one is a perfect dad, but if we are present and spend time with our kids, they know we value and love them.

Our ability to pour out blessings and love into our kids is proportionate to those things we've received from our father. In every case, whether we had a good dad or no dad, our capacity is also flawed by our humanity—our sin.

Even the greatest father out there isn't perfect. He's got shortcomings. A man without the Spirit of God moving in his life is just a mere man, limited by his human abilities.

A man filled with God's Spirit is more than a mere man—he becomes a beloved son equipped and filled with every heavenly resource he needs to pour out blessings and love into his family. Good Father, good son. God made us for so much more than just what our earthly dad could give us!

God created Adam, the first man, in His image and likeness—like Father, like son. Adam had no limitations on his life as a man, husband, and father. His identity came from his relationship with his Father. He was God's son. His capacity to have a great relationship with his wife, children, and the Father was unlimited if he continued to walk with God. His cup was full. When Adam sinned, he died spiritually and lost his supernatural connection to God as his Father. His cup was no longer full.

Do you remember when God asked Adam, "Where are you?" (Gen. 3:9b)? The Father wasn't wondering about Adam's physical location! He was asking Adam where he was spiritually. Adam had broken their "like Father, like son" relationship. He no longer looked like the Father because he had lost God's holy presence in his life. Sin had marred the image and likeness of the Father on Adam's life. Adam's sons after him would now bear even less of the Father's image on their lives. And the same is true of us, our fathers, and our children. As imperfect sons and daughters of Adam, we were all separated from the presence of God the Father, resulting in an empty cup for pouring into our families.

"The Sweat of Our Brow"

Have you ever noticed that when meeting another man for the first time after exchanging names, the next question often is "What do you do?" Many men tie their identity to what they do for a living. Why? Because of what happened in the Garden of Eden.

> "To Adam he said, Because you listened to your wife and ate from the tree about which I commanded you, 'You must not eat of it,' Cursed is the ground because of you; through painful toil you will eat of it all the days of your life. It will produce thorns and thistles for you, and you will eat the plants of the field. By the sweat of your brow you will eat your food until you return to the ground, since from it you were taken; for dust you are and to dust you will return." (Gen. 3:17–19, NIV)

Adam's relationship with God changed from an unencumbered "like Father, like son" relationship, where the presence of the Father empowered and blessed him, to a life where Adam's identity would now come from the sweat of his hard work. That is why most men today see themselves by "the sweat of their brow," or what they do for a living.

God created Adam as his first human son on planet Earth. There was no doubt about his identity before he sinned. He was God's son. After Adam sinned his identity became more about what he did, "by the sweat of his brow," rather than the blessings he received from God. Adam chose to sin against God and caused all of us men to be born outside the blessing of the Father. When we exist outside of the blessing of the Father we are "cursed" to find our identity through "the sweat of our brow." The Father sent His only Son, Jesus Christ, to end that curse.

Jesus took the curse of the sweat of our brow that Adam's sin deserved and was buried in our place so that man's end would not just be dirt but so that we could have eternal life with Him. Paul writes, "Just as we have borne the image of the man of dust, we shall also bear the image of the man of heaven" (1 Cor. 15:49).

Jesus died as the man of dust so that when we are born again, we can also bear the image of the man of heaven. When Jesus came, He restored the image of the man of heaven (Jesus) we all lost in Adam's fall. He also restored our identity as God's sons so that we can have a "like Father, like Son" relationship with our heavenly Father. When we are fathered and blessed by God we are no longer limited by the sweat of our brow.

> "This resurrection life you received from God is not a timid, grave-tending life. It's adventurously expectant, greeting God with a childlike 'What's next, Papa?'" (Rom. 8:15, MSG)

Being fathered by God like Jesus changes the way we see ourselves, from being identified by our career, "the sweat of our brow," to living out our new identity and legacy as a son. Jesus didn't only come to die in our place for the sins we've committed; He also came to restore our relationship with the Father that Adam lost. He became human like us and modeled the life of a beloved son so that "the love with which you have loved me may be in them, and I in them" (John 17:26 ESV).

The best way for us to have something to pour into our kids—to be the father our kids need and the husband our wife needs—is to have the image and likeness of Christ restored in our lives. That only happens when we enter into a relationship with the Father through the sacrifice of His Son, Jesus Christ.

So how do we do that?

> "If you confess with your mouth that Jesus is Lord and believe
> in your heart that God raised him from the dead, you will be
> saved. For with the heart one believes and is justified, and with
> the mouth one confesses and is saved." (Rom. 10:9–10)

When we are born again in Christ, the Father restores His relationship with us and adopts us as His sons and daughters in Christ. By receiving God's free gift of salvation and the forgiveness of our sins that Jesus offers us through His death, we get to partake in His resurrection from the dead—His new life—and become sons and daughters of the living God. He becomes our true good Father and we can pour into our families from a full cup—His cup!

How Do I Know the Father?

I've met hundreds of Christians over the years who called God their Father but didn't understand what it means to be fathered by God. I've met hundreds more who couldn't even call God "Father" because the wounds they received from their earthly father were too painful. "Father" was a bad word to them. They couldn't see past their father wounds and recognize their need for another Father, a greater Father, the Father they've always wanted but never knew they could have.

I received a letter from a young woman whose biological dad left her and whose stepdad beat her beginning at age 2 or 3. In addition, other father figures in her life damaged her. The true story that follows helps us understand how broken a person can become because of father wounds:

> "A friend gave me your little book on fathers, and I cannot get
> through it. I read two to three sentences and I am either stunned
> or can't see through my tears. I am a 41-year-old vibrant Chris-
> tian woman with many gifts, a master's degree, and wonderful
> friends.

Men are interested in me though I can't seem to find Mr. Right. No one would imagine this spitfire, full of charm and with a beautiful smile, would be huddled in her car last night sobbing inconsolably for four hours. I then wrote an apology letter to my family and friends but could not come up with a plan that seemed least painful.

A gigantic unfulfilled longing to know a true father's love has caught with me. Today I find myself still here on the planet. My eyes are too puffy and red to cry much more—and I am so very tired inside. Then just today I see your first newsletter appear on my iPhone.

My inside exhaustion of trying to keep going being no one's daughter is my time bomb. Last night the hope I have been trying to keep seemed to slip away, like the pin taken out of a grenade. Tired and hopeless I am reading your email and thinking, *How does he know the Father so well?* Ed, this may sound dramatic, but I want to know Him more than I want to breathe.

Dads…

I have a biological dad who left before I was born. I had a stepdad, a pastor for many decades, who adopted me but who beat me as a child repeatedly (from age 2 or 3 and on). We do not have a friendship to this day. Growing up in the church, various men involved in the Masonic abused me from age 4 to 8. These memories God is healing, but I fear I will never know the feeling of being truly *safe*, especially in the arms of a father.

As a young woman I gave my heart to the Lord at a Christian event and my whole life changed. Another pastor became a spiritual father to me; he was kind, a respected leader and very gifted with people. One night he kissed me sexually and everything changed in an instant—for the worse and never to be the same.

These events seemed to carry a target on my forehead into adulthood, leading to another handful of stories that are too much for this email.

To others, I was a wonderful youth pastor, missionary, sales rep, seminary student, fitness instructor, or marketing consultant. I have had many wonderful leaders invest professionally in me because of the gifts and calling they saw in my life, but I was never anyone's daughter.

I am still not!

How do I connect with the Father and have a relationship that is close to Him like Jesus had?

Everything feels meaningless without *knowing* the Father.

I woke up wishing I had not. I am isolating and not answering my phone when my loved one's call. I am losing hope—that I will ever know the love and care of a father. I hide away in my den and seek Him, read scripture, and pour out my heart. I just long to know Him. Why can't I seem to reach Him?

Ed, my heart aches so.

I have prayed for lepers in India, preached in jungle villages, prayed for the sick and seen them healed, but what are powers and miracles when I can't have the One who does it all?

It's like giving out brownies that everyone loves but I never can taste them myself. It is more than that; I want to know the One who made them—intimately! I don't care if I ever have another brownie. How do I know the Father in a personal way? How do you?"

We are made by God to have a loving, kind, merciful father in our story. I think it may be impossible to live a healthy life without a loving father—whether biological or spiritual. A father is more than just a biological participant. He is also the first image of who God might be: our protector, a counselor, a coach, and ultimately one who helps us discover the future for which God has made us.

The father wound is most often a wound of absence—emotional as well as physical. If God designed us to have a father, then when our father is absent it can devastate us. Simple neglect can kill the most beautiful tree in the world. Just as a plant requires active input—sun, nutrient-rich soil, water—so too we need the input of a father. Without input, we die inside.

God made us to have a relationship with our father, and no amount of friendship can replace a father's presence. I mean, the big questions inside us need answers from our dads and moms, but if our fathers are absent from our story, these questions always linger, no matter how successful our careers become.

Many men I know think the goal of their relationship with God is forgiveness. Forgiveness is important but there is much more to it. It's also developing a loving Father/son relationship and coming home to the Father's house, the place where the door of eternity is open and the welcome is always warm. This is the place from which we need to parent, the place in which we transform the absences and abuses of our earthly fathers.

This Is Who the Father Is

> "The Lord is merciful and gracious, slow to anger and abounding in steadfast love. He will not always chide, nor will he keep his anger forever. He does not deal with us according to our sins, nor repay us according to our iniquities.
>
> For as high as the heavens are above the earth, so great is his steadfast love toward those who fear him; as far as the east is from the west, so far does he remove our transgressions from us.
>
> As a father shows compassion to his children, so the Lord shows compassion to those who fear him." (Ps. 103:8-13)

If you've put your hope and trust in Jesus as your Lord and Savior, then the Father in heaven has become your Father. He loves you. And if you didn't know that, He's been waiting for you to turn to Him. He wants to have a relationship with you just as any loving father would want to have with his son or daughter.

He wants to talk to you. He wants you to speak to Him. And—get this—He's been talking to you! He's been leading and guiding you. His eye has never left you. You may not have felt it or known it, but your Father in heaven has been watching over you.

He wants to restore that "like Father, like son" relationship with you—the same relationship He has with His Son, Jesus. People looked at Jesus and knew what God the Father was like. They saw a man who loved glorifying His Dad!

Being fathered by God begins when we recognize that we have a Father in heaven and that we are His sons and daughters. When God becomes our Father, and we receive Him as His children, His presence fills our empty cups. You cannot become the good father, husband, and man you want to be without first experiencing and connecting to the power source that is the true good Father, God Himself. That is how you get a full cup.

Think of it like this: to pour out love and blessings upon your kids, you need the Father's love and blessings poured into you.

Fathering Girls?

How are you doing raising the girls in your family? I struggled to raise my girls for two main reasons. First, girls don't come with an instruction manual. My dad didn't teach me much there. Second, girls are way more complicated, because God has uniquely gifted them in ways that have confused men since the beginning of time. I wanted to be the best father I could be to my girls, but without meaning to, pouring out of an empty cup, I was unintentionally hurting them.

I was always trying to instruct and fix them—which does not work! I remember a moment when the Lord opened my eyes to learning how to connect with my girls.

I was sitting in my study working on a sermon one afternoon and my daughter Jessica, dressed in a princess outfit, showed up outside of my glass sliding door trying to get my attention. I was trying to stay focused on the task at hand when I saw Jessica trying to get my attention. As I looked at her, an internal prayer came up and I asked, "Lord, what do women want?" I didn't know the answer to this question. I loved my little girl dearly, but I didn't know what to do. My cup was empty, and I did not know how to give her what she needed.

As I was watching Jessica dancing around in her princess outfit, Mary, her younger sister, showed up in her princess outfit. Then they both started dancing outside of my office, knocking on my door trying to get my attention. They were dancing and shouting, "Daddy, look at me! Daddy, look at me!" I started praying, "Help me, Lord. What should I do? I'm busy and have so much to get done." Right in that moment the voice of the Father spoke inside of me the answer to that question of what my little girls wanted. This is what He said: "When a little girl is born, she is born with a question in her heart: Daddy, do you see me? Am I beautiful? Am I someone to be loved? If you answer that question as a father for your daughters, it will change their story forever."

A dad is the first man in a little girl's story to help her answer her biggest life questions: Am I beautiful? Am I lovable? When a girl does not get those questions answered by her father, she can struggle with her beauty and her emotional security. Leaving her with those questions unanswered, she may turn to the wrong man to get those answers.

In that moment of prayer and asking God the Father how to be a father, He started filling my empty cup by teaching me how to be a good father to my daughters and a better husband to my wife.

If you let God become your Father too, whether you had a great dad or no dad at all, He will teach you how to love the woman and children He has given you to care for.

The first thing that He showed me was to pay attention to my daughters and show affection to them when they were seeking my attention. The second thing was to cherish the emotional gifts that my daughters (and my wife) had that an ex-football player was not familiar with. In fact, I wasn't just unfamiliar; I was afraid of engaging in these tender emotions and feelings. It was foreign ground to me. You may understand why when you hear the next story.

As I was getting ready to walk out with my groomsmen, my dad came into the room to give me his words of wisdom to prepare for marrying Jill, the love of my life: "Well, son, I have little to say about women other than drama, drama, drama. That's pretty much what you get." I looked at him and said, "That's your advice just as I am ready to walk out and get married?" He smirked at me and said, "Hell, son, that's the best I got." Those probably were words his father had said to him. Even though I knew his advice wasn't the right advice, my early marriage and family struggled because I did not know how to be emotionally present for my girls and wife. It didn't feel comfortable or safe because my dad never modeled being emotionally present to me. I even remember repeating my dad's words to my wife when I thought she was acting too emotional. I blurted, "Drama, drama, drama." Like father, like son, I unintentionally hurt my loved one because my cup was truly empty.

The third thing I started doing after the Father spoke to me was taking my daughters out for daddy date night to confirm my love and strengthen my relationship with them. I worked hard at trying to become the kind of man I wanted my daughters to choose one day.

When a daughter doesn't have a father's love to help her discover her beauty and her self-worth as a chosen woman of God, she is not clear about who she is. If she doesn't feel loved by her father, the one who should love her the most, she will not see herself as someone who carries much value. Because she feels unloved by her dad, she will accept boys who don't know how to love her. As a result, she can choose bad boys instead of men of honor because the first man in her story, her father, didn't help her discover her value and beauty.

As you can see from my story above, in my early days I was one of those dads who don't know how to connect to their daughters. My inability to be emotionally present with my oldest daughter resulted in some very difficult times in her life. What happens when you try your best and still make mistakes as a dad? It is never too late to be the father your kids need you to be. Because of my new connection with the Father, I could become the father I needed to be. Even though I didn't start out as a good father with my daughter Jessica, as I learned to receive from the Father, I became a better father. As I received from the Father, I was able to pass on the blessing I received to my daughter Jessica, which helped to heal her wounds from my mistakes of the past.

Below is a letter my oldest, Jessica, wrote to me during a hard time in her life.

"I'm writing you this letter because I wanted to thank you for being my safe place and to share with you the most impactful moment you had in my life. Ever since I was a little girl, I knew that I could go to you for advice. To me, you were the voice of God until I could hear the Father's voice for myself. Through my hardest times, you've listened to my challenges and heart-breaks and always pointed me to the Father.

As I got older, you stopped answering my questions and would ask me, "Well what do you think God is telling you?" To which I would answer, "Well, nothing because I came to you first." You would laugh and I would get so frustrated because I knew you had the answer but wanted me to find it out for myself. You trained me to never doubt the Father's voice in my life. You taught me to read the Word and get quiet. I am forever grateful for this practice in my life.

My greatest moment of influence from you, however, was your act of love in one of the hardest seasons of my life. I was a sophomore in college and got stuck in a physical relationship with a "pretender," as you would call him. He stole my virgin-ity and the weight of the sin kept me in a dark place, somehow unable to walk away or talk to anyone about it. After three short months, I ended up finding out I was pregnant and knew that it was time to talk to you.

At that point, I couldn't hear the Father's voice because the thick, empty lull of my sins deafened me. I knew that what had happened was wrong, but I wasn't able to see or hear much of anything from God. Heartbroken and ashamed, I somehow worked up the courage to plan a family meeting. In front of you, Mom and my siblings, I wept as I shared my deep dark secret with the ones I loved most. I looked up from telling my story only to see my family weeping along with me.

Without hesitation, Dad, you wiped the tears from your eyes, looked at me, and said, "You are my beloved daughter and I will always be here for you. It doesn't matter what you've done. I forgive you. The Father loves you, and I will be here for you for every step of this journey." You then leaped out of your seat, walked across the room, and held me. I wept in your arms for what felt like an eternity. My heart began to finally come to a place of rest and I felt the burden on my shoulders start to melt away. When I deserved punishment, you met me with an act of compassionate love. It was an embrace that I will never forget.

From that point on you discipled me and were a huge part of my journey back to the Father's house. You spent your mornings praying with me and speaking over the child in my womb. You challenged me to fill my heart with God's Word. You helped me set boundaries with the child's father when I couldn't figure out how to lay down the line on my own. You and Mom cared for me and truly showed me how much the Father loved me, without even having to think about it. Well, that's how it seemed at least.

A month later, you were the one to hold my hand as I screamed in pain and fear during my three-hour labor and miscarriage. We wept so many times together that night holding each other.

In my greatest moments of sorrow, you were there for me. It's because of your sacrificial love and presence in a moment when I knew I didn't deserve it that I survived in the wilderness and could reconnect to my heavenly Father again. Thank you, Dad, for this moment and so many more.

Your favorite oldest daughter, Jessica"

This letter is a treasure to me because it shows the power that a father has to either help or hurt his children. It's devastating to learn that your actions have hurt the daughter you love and promised to protect. And it's also powerful to be a part of healing your daughter's story that shapes her for the rest of her life. It's easy to see from this letter the difference it makes to pour from a cup that is being filled by God the Father rather than a cup left empty by the mistakes fathers have passed down since Adam.

In summary, to be the husband that your wife needs and the father your daughters need (or that your sons need), here are four things you need to do:

1. Spend time with them. There is no substitute for time with Dad. Time is your most valuable asset; spend it on them.

2. Pay attention to what they're saying, doing, or thinking when you're with them.

3. Show them affection and tell them you love them frequently, highlighting the things you love about them.

4. Tell your wife and daughter how beautiful, intelligent, and capable they are.

A husband's and father's words have great power to name, bless, and call out the gifts and beauty of the girls in your life.

Do the same for your boys. Your son's biggest questions are, "What does my dad really think about me? Does he believe I have what it takes to be a man? Does my dad trust me?" Tell them the things you admire about them—their gifts, their strengths—that you believe in them, and that you are there to help them discover who God has made them to be.

When you consistently do those things for your wife and kids, they will feel your blessing and know that their father sees them and celebrates who God has made them to be. That is what it means to be present for your family!

What a difference it would make to the lives of our daughters and wives if we were to become the husband our wife needs and the father our children need. We would change the world of our wives and children, wouldn't we? Writing these words has reminded me of all the moments I missed seeing my daughters and celebrating my wife's beauty. I have learned that it is never too late to begin again by learning from the Father how to become the husband and father my family needs. So what is the secret to being fathered by God?

Learning to Receive

As I mentioned earlier, I like to call allowing oneself to be fathered by God the Receiving Principle. It's the secret to being a great man, husband, and father. Our ability to be the father and husband our family needs depends upon our willingness to receive the blessing of the Father through Jesus Christ. The Receiving Principle is all about following what the Father is doing, the way Jesus did. When we are receiving like Jesus did, we don't take the lead on our own. Rather, we are always looking for what the Father is doing so that we can do likewise.

> "So Jesus said to them, 'Truly, truly, I say to you, the Son can do nothing of his own accord, but only what he sees the Father doing. For whatever the Father does, that the Son does likewise.'" (John 5:19)

This is counterintuitive to the way most of us live our lives. We have been taught that whatever we want in life we have to earn through the sweat of our brow. Receiving God's grace without earning it is especially hard for us men, because most of us have been raised in performance-driven systems where only winners get the rewards.

When Jill and I were first married, I got stuck trying to have a winning season with her, instead of just loving Jill for who she was. I was measuring our relationship like the scoreboard at a football game, hoping Jill would measure up to my standards as a wife or hoping she would not throw a penalty flag because I did something wrong again.

Performance-driven systems don't work in relationships because performance is all about the reward or the end goal instead of being about loving the other person the way Jesus loved the church.

Performance-driven relationships compete, with each party keeping score. For example, dialogs like these play out in many marriages: "I'm such a good husband, so why doesn't she show more respect for my hard work?" Or, "I work so hard to take care of the kids, so why doesn't he show me more attention?" Or, "Kids, how many times have I told you not to do that? Don't make me come over there."

The focus is all on doing to receive love. Performance-based love also doesn't work because it naturally produces fear of what will happen when we aren't able to perform or measure up in our relationships. And we will all fail to measure up in our relationships more often than we would like. Performance-based relationships are the foundational concept in divorce: "If you are not the good husband (or wife) I want you to be, then I will leave you. See you later!" Performance-based relationships are not true loving relationships because they create fear and insecurity.

As a professional football player, I had lived my whole life, from Pop Warner to the NFL, focused on performance. It's how I measured everything. When I married Jill, she was the first person who truly liked me for who I was rather than what I did. She would tell me all the things she loved about me repeatedly—not that there weren't moments when she pointed out things that hurt or disappointed her. But in her heart she not only loved me, but she also really liked me.

I had a knee replacement surgery about 10 years ago and Jill picked me up from my tenth doctor appointment. I wasn't able to drive at that time. I looked at her and said, "I'm sorry, babe, that you have to drive my big butt everywhere and I haven't been able to be there more for you." She looked over at me and said, "What are you talking about? This is the most romantic time in our entire relationship!" My jaw hit the ground.

What about those sunset dinners on Maui, or those mountain-top experiences of romance? That's how I measured romance. She glanced over at me and answered, "You still don't get it, do you? I just love being with you. I like you, Ed! You're my best friend; you're my lover; you're the man God gave me and I just love spending time with you." My wife was teaching me the meaning of unconditional love: no performance required, no making the team, no getting cut, no losing your job to someone who performed better.

Here's what John said about God's perfect love:

> "There is no fear in love, but perfect love casts out fear. For fear has to do with punishment, and whoever fears has not been perfected in love" (1 John 4:18).

When you're loved by someone without fear, you experience the way God loves us. Jesus broke the power of fear in love by dying on the cross and taking the punishment we deserved for our sin. Jill understood how to love me and like me, because she first learned to receive God's love without fear for herself. His love for her taught Jill to love me without using fear. She was the first girl who knew who she was and who was secure enough to love me God's way.

Now I faced one of my biggest hurdles: learning how to receive Jill's love without trying to earn it! When you are performing for love, you are keeping score. When you are keeping score, you are not receiving! When you are not receiving, you are not learning to love your family God's way. God said, "It is not good for a man to be alone." Adam would have never had someone to love and receive from without Eve. Could it be that God gave you a wife to teach you how to receive and give love? I know He has for me, and I am so grateful for the woman He gave me. Because Jesus became the offering for our sin, we can now enjoy the Father's goodness, love, and grace as His sons and daughters. We can enjoy the blessing of the Father not because we earned it or performed for it but because God the Father chose us to love as His children.

"What marvelous love the Father has extended to us! Just look
at it—we're called children of God! That's who we really are."
(1 John 3:1, MSG)

We can't earn God's love by trying to be a good person or by performing and
following a list of religious rules. God's love is marvelous because He offers it
to us for free and we get to choose how much of His love we receive. The more
of the Father's love we receive, the more we become the children He has called
us to be.

The question is, will you receive it? It's not a one-time transaction. If you
step into this relationship with your heavenly Father through the sacrifice of His
Son, Jesus, then you will receive all that you need to become the man, father, and
husband you've always wanted to be—and so much more.

I started learning how to receive from God and an amazing thing started
happening to me as a father: God's love toward me started turning my heart
back to my children. I had spent so much of my adult life trying to arrive that
my children were starving for time with me. They are all a blessing and bring
me joy every day. I'm not always the greatest father. I've made a lot of mistakes!
But the secret I've discovered to being the father and husband my family needs
is the Receiving Principle. When we open our hearts to receive from God, He
fills us to become the man, husband, and father God has called us to be. When
we receive from God, allowing Him to fill our cups, then we have something
incredible to pour out into our wife and children.

"So, what do you think? With God on our side like this, how
can we lose? If God didn't hesitate to put everything on the line
for us, embracing our condition and exposing himself to the
worst by sending his own Son, is there anything else he wouldn't
gladly and freely do for us?" (Rom. 8:31–32, MSG)

Imagine for a moment that your cup, which keeps getting poured out each
day into your family, needs refilling. This is the Receiving Principle. It's an

ongoing process. You won't wake up as a perfect dad one day, and your kids will not become amazing in one day either. There are no magic potions in receiving the blessing of the Father. As you receive, as you open yourself up to receive more and more from your Father in heaven, you will become the father that your kids need because you will pour into them what they need from a full cup. As you set the example of receiving from God, and if you are as patient as the Father has been with you, your kids will receive the Father's blessing themselves.

Do you have a question about something your kid is going through right now? Maybe you're not sure how to handle a particular situation. God will show you how to handle it as you become a man of blessing! And that, my friends, is how you become the father your kids need.

Throughout this book, we will discuss more and more specifics regarding how to put yourself in the place of receiving the blessing of the Father. We will look at examples from the Bible, such as Moses and Peter, to see how God fathered them, how He spoke to them, and how they received from Him and became the men God called them to be. We will walk through receiving the blessing of the Father together.

When we learn to receive the Father's blessing every day, He fills our cup so we can become the father and husband God has called us to be.

Personal Insights

1. Did your father do things that hurt you when you were growing up?

2. Did you promise not to do the same things to your kids?

3. How did your father's parenting style affect your parenting style?

4. Are you spending enough time with your wife and children?

5. What is the Receiving Principle?

Key Takeaways

Listen to these words for you from Jesus:

> "What father among you, if his son asks for a fish, will instead
> give him a serpent; or if he asks for an egg, will give him a scor-
> pion? If you then, who are evil, know how to give good gifts to
> your children, how much more will the heavenly Father give
> the Holy Spirit to those who ask him!" (Luke 11:11-13)

God is a good Father who wants to give you good gifts. He is the perfect Father, whose love, wisdom, and skills are far superior to any human. God wants to fill your cup to overflowing so that you have more than enough to get through your day and to pour into your wife and kids. God wants to father us and give us the good gift of His Holy Spirit. He wants to transform us into the husband and father He called us to be, back into His image.

How To's

1. **According to the principle of "like father, like son," how can we be fathered by God?**

    Repent of your sins, confess with your mouth that Jesus' sacrifice has paid for all your sins, and receive the adoption as a child of God through Jesus Christ.

    > "If you confess with your mouth that Jesus is Lord and believe
    > in your heart that God raised him from the dead, you will be
    > saved. For with the heart one believes and is justified, and with
    > the mouth, one confesses and is saved." (Rom. 10:9–10)

    Being fathered by God begins when we fully receive the fact that we are His sons and daughters and spend time daily with Him reading His Word and talking with Him in prayer.

"For all who are led by the Spirit of God are sons of God. For you did not receive the spirit of slavery to fall back into fear, but you have received the Spirit of adoption as sons, by whom we cry, "Abba! Father!" The Spirit himself bears witness with our spirit that we are children of God." (Rom. 8:14–16)

When you put your hope and trust in Jesus as your Lord and Savior, then the Father in heaven has become your Father. He loves you. That is the beginning of a new "like Father, like son" relationship. He's been waiting for you to turn to Him. He wants to have a relationship with you just as any loving father would have with his son or daughter.

He wants to talk to you. He wants you to speak to Him. And—get this—He's been talking to you! He's been leading and guiding you. His eye has never left you. You may not have felt it or known it, but your Father in heaven has been watching over you. Being fathered by God begins when we fully receive the fact that we are His sons and daughters and spend time daily with Him reading His Word.

When God becomes our Father, and we receive Him as His children, His presence fills us, which gives us everything we need to fill our empty cups. You cannot become the good father and husband you want to be without first experiencing and connecting to the power source that is the true good Father, God Himself.

**To help you connect to the power source every day
please access our free daily devotional here:**
blessingofthefather.com/daily-devotional

2.   How do you receive the blessing of the Father?

We have to be humble enough to admit we can't fix ourselves without God's help. We have to receive God's mercy by asking for forgiveness. We have to forgive those around us, especially our wives and children, because they need God's mercy too.

This is the Receiving Principle. We can't earn it; we have to receive God's blessing, which is His love, mercy, and forgiveness. Receiving is especially hard for men because it was never modeled in their families that receiving help was a value. Most of us learned in performance-driven systems that only winners get the rewards. Most of us were taught to fix our problems ourselves. We weren't taught to ask for help. We were taught to give help.

When Jesus became the sacrifice for our sins, we were given the opportunity to receive forgiveness. Because Jesus became the offering for our sin, we can now freely enjoy the Father's goodness and grace as His sons and daughters. We can enjoy the blessing of the Father.

> "Let us then with confidence draw near to the throne of grace,
> that we may receive mercy and find grace to help in time of
> need." (Heb. 4:16)

Our ability to be the father and husband our family needs depends upon our willingness to receive the blessing of the Father through Jesus Christ. When we receive the blessing of the Father into our hearts and minds and allow God to father us the way He fathered His Son, Jesus, our cup will be full. We will be able to pour into our wife and children that same love, mercy, and forgiveness the Father has poured into us.

**To help you learn to pour love mercy and
forgiveness into to your wife and children.**
We are offering you a free ebook of *The Difference a Father Makes*
https://www.blessingofthefather.com/freebook
Take advantage of our free offer.
It will change the way you think about being a father.

Prayer

Father, I need You. I need You to fill my cup, to give me more of You. Thank You for making a way for me to be transformed into Your image. Forgive me for the times I have tried to do it on my own. I have little to give without You. Fill me again with Your Holy Spirit so that I can become the man, husband, and father You have created me to be! I want to be just like You. I want to love the way You love Jesus. In Jesus' name, amen!

CHAPTER 2

RECEIVING: YOUR CALLING

A man can receive nothing unless it has been given to him from heaven ... He must increase, but I must decrease.

John 3:27, 30

These were the words of John the Baptist when challenged by his disciples regarding the ministry of Jesus surpassing his own. John knew that his calling could only be fulfilled by receiving everything he needed from God. John also knew that he would have to decrease in order for Jesus to increase. What is God calling you to?

Receiving My Calling

During my junior year, while playing football for Youngstown State University, an overzealous freshman dove for a loose ball and ran straight into my left knee. This resulted in the tearing of all three major ligaments, which needed surgery the next day. I was told that it would be likely that I would not play football—my lifelong dream—ever again.

During that heartbreak, while waiting for surgery, the Lord met me through our team chaplain. I received Christ as my Savior that day and discovered the following day, much to my surprise (and the shock of the surgeons), that the torn ligaments were reattached in my knee and that God had healed me—no surgery required.

I was so overwhelmed by the miraculous healing that I took a walk and asked God what He wanted me to do with my life. I did not understand if God would even reply. I had no context for talking to God or even prayer. I didn't even own a Bible.

Suddenly, I felt God speaking and whispering to my heart.

He said, "Ed, I want you to fulfill your dream of playing professional football."

It shocked me. I lifted my head up (I assumed God must be up in the clouds somewhere) and said, "If I knew You were this cool, I would have gotten saved a long time ago! What kind of God are You that You would give a broken man like me his dream?"

God responded, "Ed, who do you think put that dream inside of you? But when I call for it back, give it up."

I was so enraptured by the goodness of God to give me my dream that I did not understand what He meant when He said that He would "call for it back." I only knew that God was good. He was the giver of dreams. And He was speaking to me!

After my moment with God, I called Bill, the team pastor, on the phone, to tell him what happened at the hospital. I told him about the doctor's report that my ligaments had been reattached and that my knee was healed. He said, "You're kidding, right?"

I said, "No, Bill, I'm not! Your prayer for me yesterday not only opened my heart to Jesus but it also healed my knee so I can fulfill my dream."

Bill said, "Eddie, I have never seen anyone healed like that from one of my prayers. That's amazing!" He called his wife, Donna, into the room, and I could hear her in the background praising God for what Jesus had just done.

I then asked Bill, "What am I supposed to do now that I am a Christian? I don't have a Bible yet."

He quickly said, "I'll bring one to you."

I then asked, "What else do you want me to do?"

He said, "Do you still have that little booklet I gave you from Bill Bright called *The Four Spiritual Laws?*"

I said, "I do."

"I want you to take that book to the quad where the students hang out for lunch and find someone and lead them to Christ. Just like I did with you!"

I responded, "Okay, I will."

I walked into the quad area and looked around for someone to share Jesus with. I was nervous, fearing someone would ask me a question I didn't know the answer to. I saw a cute girl from my physics class, thinking to myself, *Why wouldn't God want to save a cute girl?* Karen looked at me and said, "Hey, Ed, what's up?"

I replied, "Have you heard of the four spiritual laws?"

She said, "No. What are those?"

I sat down across from her and started reading the book to her. I started getting nervous and stopped looking up at her and just buried my head and read the book. After about five minutes of reading, I came to the prayer of dedication for someone willing to give their life to Christ. I asked her to pray this prayer with me, "Lord Jesus."

I heard her repeat, "Lord Jesus." I looked up. Her head was bowed and tears were rolling down her cheeks. The same Jesus I met the night before was there loving Karen.

I continued the prayer: "I need You. Thank You for dying on the cross for my sins. I open the door of my life and receive You as my Savior and Lord. Thank You for forgiving my sins and giving me eternal life. Take control of the throne of my life. Make me the kind of person You want me to be. In Jesus' name. Amen!"

Both of us were weeping as the presence of the One who had died for us filled our hearts. I was so honored to be there watching the miracle of someone being born again, just like I had been the day before. God was teaching me that miracles can happen if I step out in faith and reach out to someone who has not encountered Jesus for themselves. I am not the one doing the saving; Jesus is. My job was to invite Karen to meet Jesus for herself, and she sure did. She was never the same from that day forward.

I jumped up from my encounter with Karen and gave her a high five and then made my way to the payphone to call Bill to tell him about Karen giving her life to Christ. I got on the phone and said, "Hey, Bill. Guess what? I got a girl …" Bill interrupted me, saying, "Eddie, I wasn't asking you to get a girl."

I jumped in, "No, I meant that I read that book you gave me, *The Four Spiritual Laws*, to a girl named Karen. And she just prayed with me to receive Jesus in her life! It was amazing!"

Bill asked, "You just led someone to Christ?"

I said, "Yes, I did. You told me to go and lead someone to Christ. So I did!"

Bill responded, "I'm just a little shocked and overjoyed that you were able to do it for the first time. I think that God has given you the gift of evangelism." The rest of that year I wore out reading that little book to my friends and saw over a hundred and twenty-five of my classmates at Youngstown State University receive Jesus into their life and be saved. Not only was God calling me to be a football player, but He was also calling me to lead people to Jesus.

Paul wrote about his calling, "… when He who had set me apart before I was born, and who called me by his grace, was pleased to reveal his Son to me, in order that I might preach him among the Gentiles" (Gal. 1:15–16).

God the Father has set all of us apart for a purpose He has made us to fulfill. It is the Father's pleasure to reveal His Son to us so we can fulfill His calling on our life. Like Paul, when we are able to declare that "God set me apart before I was born," then that is a powerful moment for us as men. Do you know what God set you apart for?

Years later, I was living out my dream through five seasons in the NFL. I played against great Pro-Bowl defensive linemen like All-Pros Mean Joe Greene and Joe Klecko and practiced against linebacker Lawrence Taylor, one of the all-time greatest defensive players in NFL history.

I was drafted by the New York Jets. On the very first play of the first pre-season game I played for the Jets, I had to block Mean Joe Greene. He was one of the all-time greats and was the most feared defensive lineman in the NFL. I remember breaking the huddle and turning to face him, all six foot four and 276 pounds of cat-like quickness staring me down. I grabbed the ball and snapped it to our quarterback, Richard Todd. I got a quick step on Joe and was able to get underneath his shoulder pads and push him over and ended up landing on the chest of one of my heroes. I was thinking, *I'm the man. I just blocke• Mean Joe Greene!* Joe looked at me and said, "Hey, rookie, this is pre-season; don't hurt me." I realized at that moment that this battle with Mean Joe was not over.

Toward the end of that series we ran another play and I had to block Joe again. This time he jumped around me like a giant cat, ran into the backfield, picked up our quarterback, Richard Todd, and drove him into the turf. I heard the coach scream my last name from the sidelines, "McGlasson," which is not a good sign. I dusted myself off to walk back to the huddle.

Joe was walking my way and looked at me and said, "Hey, rookie!"

I said, "Yeah, Joe?"

He said, "I just wanted you to know who I am."

That was my introduction to one of the greatest defensive linemen in the NFL. I played for one year with the Jets behind All-Pro center Joe Fields. During my time with the Jets I was able to lead a number of players to Christ. In fact, during the season I had daily open debates in the locker room with five-time All-Pro offensive tackle Marvin Powell, who was a Muslim at the time. Most of the team heard our debates and observed my defense of Jesus. I was learning how to share the love of Jesus in a firm yet kind and gentle way to a group of men trained to be warriors.

I was cut by the Jets, and the Los Angeles Rams needed a center and picked me up to join the team. I remember my first moments with the team as All-Pro center Rich Saul met me in the locker room. "Hey, Eddie Mac, it's great to have you on the team. They brought you to play center and back me up and to be our long snapper. Let's take a knee and pray that God uses us to reach every one of our teammates for Jesus!" It was an honor for me to take a knee with Rich; he was modeling with his actions his deep commitment to giving his life in service to Jesus. As it turned out, God had called Rich and me to play football, but He also called us to lead NFL players to Christ.

During training camp in my second season I was released from the Rams and picked up by the New York Giants. My favorite memories with the Giants were my interactions with my teammates sharing my love and faith in Jesus. George Martin, Bill Currier, Joe Morris and I started praying together for our teammates to meet Jesus, and by the end of the season, we saw over 30 of our teammates decide for Christ. George was the starting defensive tackle who amassed 90 sacks in his career, played on the Super Bowl XXI winning team, and eventually became the Executive Director of the NFL Alumni Association. Bill was the starting defensive back and was one of the most consistent players on the team. He went on to a career in coaching. Joe was a 5' 7" Pro Bowl package of muscle and speed. He was a key player in the Giants' 1987 Super Bowl XXI win. He rushed for 67 yards, caught four passes for 20 yards, and scored a touchdown in the game.

After games we would go out to the middle of the field, take a knee, and pray together. We saw many lives change after they encountered Jesus, just like mine had.

When the Giants won Super Bowl XXI, even though I was in full-time ministry, I was invited to the after-party with the Giants. George Martin saw me standing in the lobby and said, "Hey, Eddie Mack, how are you doing, man? Do you want to come up to my room? A couple of us are going to go up and pray to thank the Lord for this amazing day." George was a guy who quickly gave the glory to the Lord for whatever he accomplished. We went up to his room and I wanted to talk about the game, how well he played, what it felt like to play in the Super Bowl. I peppered him with questions. George stopped and looked at me and said, "I guess that winning the Super Bowl is one of the greatest experiences you can have as an athlete. But it really doesn't come close to what you get to do leading people to Christ."

While I was still with the Giants, George joined me in the off season to minister to 500 inmates at the Montana State Prison. We saw approximately 300 men stand up and give their lives to Christ that day. Those are moments you never forget.

I had been sensing that God was leading me into something new, but I wasn't ready to give up on my dream of playing football. I thought my being a football player was my calling and identity. God called me to fulfill my childhood dream, but He was now calling me to decrease so that I could learn to receive His ultimate calling on my life to serve Him as a beloved son. God was asking me to decrease what I wanted to do so that Jesus could increase what He wanted to do.

I Must Decrease

In 1983 the Philadelphia Eagles invited me to training camp. I had just spent my off-season sharing my testimony with high school students and inviting them to come forward and receive Jesus into their life. In San Antonio, Texas, we saw over 20,000 young people come forward to give their lives to Christ in our two-week high school outreach campaign with Fellowship of Christian Athletes and local churches in the San Antonio area. I had thought my dream was just about playing football, but God had a much bigger calling for me.

One night at training camp I couldn't sleep, so I snuck out of the dormitory while the other players were sleeping and went for a walk. I was walking down the middle of a soccer field when I heard God's voice inside of me say, "Ed, I want you to give up football and preach the gospel."

I immediately tried to negotiate with the Lord: "But, God, don't You know how much I am doing and giving to the church?" God didn't respond to my attempt at negotiation, and I headed back to my room.

The next day during practice, we were working on pass blocking drills, and it was my turn. I lined up in front of All-Pro nose guard Charlie Johnson, known as Big Hands Johnson, a giant of a man, 6' 3" and 310 pounds. My job was to block him, like I had done many times. Imagine trying to stop a train engine from getting past you. He was explosive and strong, and I did my best to block him, until I heard my ligaments rip in my right knee. My knee exploded on the inside as I twisted and turned in excruciating pain. I fell face down on the ground under the weight of Big Hands on top of me.

The team doctor examined me and the look on his face told me everything. The coaches moved the huddle so that the doctor and training staff could put me on a gurney and take me to the hospital. They ran tests on my knee to see if I needed surgery.

The next day, the doctor came into my room and told me that I hadn't torn any ligaments and didn't need surgery. They immediately put me into rehab but I could tell that something was still not right. I feared that they were not telling me the truth and were planning to cut me. One week later they confirmed my greatest fear—they cut me from the team, even though my knee was still injured. It devastated me. It had never occurred to me that the team might release me while injured. I went back home to set up an appointment with my old team doctor from the Los Angeles Rams, Dr. Clarence Shields. He did the same kind of test and told me that I needed surgery right away. The next day I went under the knife again.

When I woke up in my room, my wife and my best friend, Brian Holloway, were in my room. Brian and I had been friends since high school and went to the NFL together. He looked at me: "You know, brother, God has called you to much bigger things than being an NFL football player. If you were to have a long career, you would deprive hundreds of thousands of people of coming to know the Jesus you introduced me to. It's time for you to step into your calling and release the gift that God has given you."

A few moments later Dr. Shields came into the room to visit me and said, "Ed, the surgery went great. You could still go out and play if you want to, but God has something bigger for you to do, and it's not the NFL. I think He's called you to be a preacher."

I knew both of them were speaking the truth to me. But it was a truth I didn't want to hear. I was still deeply attached to my identity as a pro football player because that is who I thought I was. It is a fearful place for a man when his identity is centered on what he does for a living and he loses his job. I had lost my identity and didn't know who I was. I had lost my confidence in myself to be a success at something other than football.

Remember when I wrote that God wanted me to fulfill my dream of playing professional football but that He had also said, "When I call for it back, give it up"? Well, He was asking me to give my football dream back to Him and receive His calling to lead people to Jesus.

The Path Called Dumb and Dumber

The next lesson I learned when receiving my calling is what happens when you resist God's calling.

I literally felt like I was drowning, grabbing for anything to help me out of this time because I didn't know how I would support my family being in the ministry. I came up with a "How to get rich quick scheme when God calls you into the ministry." My scheme would have earned top honors at the Dumb and Dumber Academy. I started a lobster fishing business. My only experience with lobsters was them being sliced down the middle with garlic and butter. Forrest Gump had it right when he said, "Stupid is as stupid does." I had zero background in commercial fishing and no particular connection to the sea, yet there I was, ready to motor out into the deep blue and prove that I could provide for myself. My wife came down to the docks to send me off, shaking her head back and forth, saying, "Ed, I've prayed that God wouldn't kill you for being so dumb."

As I headed out toward Catalina Island off the coast of Los Angeles, California, I had no way of knowing that the El Niño storm system that year would bring big winter storms to the island. One evening while I was out on my boat, a big storm blew in, and with each towering set of waves, my lobster pots were pushed closer and closer to the cliffs on the back side of the island.

I arrived at my fishing area just as the sun was rising; and after eight hours of bone-crushing work, I saw my last three lobster pots tangled together near the cliffs at the water's edge. I had to pull up my pots and move them out to deeper water so they wouldn't be destroyed by the crashing of the waves. I also had to time my trips inside the sets of twenty-foot waves that were roaring in every five minutes. I slipped in with my hook to snatch my last three pots. However, in my tired and frantic state, I didn't notice that the three pot lines had wrapped together. They drifted under my boat and into my spinning propeller. Within seconds, the lines wrapped around my prop and choked my motor to a stop.

Suddenly, my boat was anchored to the bottom in sixty feet of water with a fresh set of huge waves heading toward me. What happened next seemed like it took forever but probably lasted mere seconds. The same voice that called me to trust God in Philadelphia now sternly said, "Preach or drown?"

God's protection and provision always come to us in the things He calls us to, but not in the things we call ourselves to. In that instant, I realized how foolish I was to run from the love and protection of God's calling and put myself in harm's way.

I shouted to the heavens, "Okay, I'll preach the gospel and go anywhere You send me—but save me from this!" I took my boat out of gear and restarted my engine. What looked like the biggest wave of the day was bearing down on me as I pushed the throttle forward and proclaimed, "In the name of Jesus!" My engine sputtered as my rope-tangled propeller strained for revolutions. Suddenly I heard a large snap as the prop cut through the ropes. I quickly turned the boat into a huge wave and piloted my little boat up the face of a wave that seemed as tall and steep as a cliff. I was screaming at the top of my lungs, "Jesus!"

I barely made it outside the breaking waves, knowing I had to get into the water to un-foul my propeller if I wanted to make it back home. I grabbed my Rambo survival knife and jumped into the cold winter water. Have you ever tried to swim, cry, cut, and repent at the same time? Trust me, it's not easy. The swelling waves and the boat's lurching made it impossible for me to reach the propeller. As I feared, hypothermia was setting in. I grabbed the fouled rope with

Sell your books at
sellbackyourBook.com!
Go to sellbackyourBook.com
and get an instant price
quote. We even pay the
shipping - see what your old
books are worth today!

Inspected By: ana_esparza

00066821409

0006682

1409

c-2,
S-3

my left hand and then a badly timed swing with my knife missed the rope and gashed my left hand instead! Blood started pumping out of my hand while the theme of *Jaws* played in my head. Afraid of being a main course at a shark dinner party, my paranoia caused every wave to look like a fin. My lips started shaking from the cold and I knew I had only a few moments left. Choking on salt water, I struggled to say, "Help me, God! I don't want to die like this!"

I composed myself enough to attempt a final cut with my knife, and this time I sliced through the rope, freeing it from the propeller. However, because of my haste when I jumped off the side, my swim plank was still inside the boat. My climb back into the boat over the jagged edges of the pots shredded my chest. Convinced I would die of some ghastly infection, I grabbed the only antiseptic on board—rubbing alcohol—and poured it all over my chest. I let out one of the most powerful primal screams in history! That night there was a report on the island that a Sasquatch was heard yowling at sundown!

Still alive, I motored to the harbor and docked my boat. All I could think about was getting to a phone and calling my wife to tell her that I was alive—and finished with my lobster-fishing gig.

I felt like Jonah in the Bible who God asked to go preach to the people of Nineveh and instead went in a different direction; I went lobster fishing. Sometimes we find it difficult to receive the Father's blessing even after He has demonstrated that He is right there by our side.

How many of you have been called by God to do something that seemed beyond your ability? Perhaps you didn't feel the call to the ministry but you felt God's call to be a great dad when you held your child in your arms for the first time. Or you felt an urge to be a better man when you met your wife, certain you could leave your past behind only to discover that your inner critic, or maybe a past voice from your earthly father, speaks up and says, "No way. You don't know how to do that." Or, "You are not good enough for that." Or maybe even, "You will never amount to anything." Some of you heard your heavenly Father whispering to you and thought, *Okay! I will ⋅o it, but I want to ⋅o it my way,* and you tripped on your first step just like I did with the lobster-fishing business.

You aren't alone. God never wastes our missteps to teach us like a father does to a son the lessons we will need to learn to face the future God has made us for. God has called every one of us to do something beyond our ability—to be a great father, husband, and man.

When God calls us to do things beyond our human ability, often we stumble and fall short. When we stumble, it's easy to believe the lie that it must be because we can't do it. But falling short of perfection is part of being human. That's why we need to be fathered by God and continuously filled with the Holy Spirit to do the things the Father is calling us to do. You will never be a perfect man, husband, or dad 100 percent of the time. But that doesn't mean you aren't cut out for your calling as a husband or father. It just means you're human and you need the Father to give you what you need—and what you don't have—to do the job He's called you to do. There was one more lesson the Father taught me that day with lobster fishing.

I motored back to my back-bay mooring at Catalina. I jumped in my dingy, still wearing my bloodstained T-shirt, and rowed to the main dock so I could call my wife. It was a quarter-mile walk to the telephone, and the wind started picking up. Before I knew it, I was in the midst of a thunderstorm. As I headed toward the phone, I noticed that there was a large herd of buffalo in my way on the road. (The Wrigley family donated parts of Catalina Island to save them from extinction.) My grandfather used to say to me, "Don't buffalo me, Ed." I did not understand what he meant until that day in the middle of a thunderstorm as I stood in front of about three hundred buffalo.

One buffalo closest to me started running full speed toward me. I wanted to run away, but my feet were frozen. I stood my ground, and when he got within ten feet of me, he slammed on the brakes and started snorting at me. I thought he looked like the legendary middle linebacker Dick Butkus; my football instincts took over, and I started charging at *him*! He ran away, and my path to the phone— and to the rest of my life—was clear.

It wasn't until later that I learned buffaloes are scared of humans, but they charge you to test you and to find out if you are afraid. If you run away, it gives the buffalo courage to keep charging, but if you hold your ground, the buffalo knows who is boss! I could almost see Jesus sitting with His Father on the throne, sending one buffalo after another to teach me a lesson I would never forget.

He is the one who empowers me to fulfill the calling on my life, and if I just stand in front of whatever charges me, He will take care of me: "Therefore, take up the whole armor of God, that you may be able to withstand in the evil day, and having done all, to *stand* firm" (Eph. 6:13, emphasis mine).

After I got home from my crazy experience, I sat on the couch with my first-born son, Edward, in my lap and said, "Okay, Father, I'm in the ministry now!"

My fear drove me to the sea, but it took the Father's love to bring me home. Home was where the love and blessing of the Father were waiting for me so that I could bless my family and those He brings my way. God was calling me to live from His love rather than my own resources, becoming the man that He was calling me to be.

Receiving the Call to Become a New Person

Moses was born during a time when the children of Israel were living in the land of Egypt as slaves. When the Israelites continued to multiply and grow stronger, Pharaoh feared their numbers were growing too large and becoming a threat to his kingdom. He instituted a population control measure and commanded that all male children born to the Israelite mothers be killed and thrown into the Nile River.

Moses' mother hid him for three months. Finally, when she could no longer protect him, she placed him in a basket floating on the Nile River, hoping that someone would find him and save his life. In an incredible story, Moses was found in the river by Pharaoh's daughter: "She saw the basket among the reeds and sent her servant woman, and she took it. When she opened it, she saw the child, and behold, the baby was crying. She took pity on him and said, 'This is one of the Hebrews' children'" (Exod. 2:5b-6). In a remarkable turn of events, Pharaoh's daughter then hired and paid Moses' mother to nurse her own son. And when he was weaned, Pharaoh's daughter adopted him.

They raised Moses in the palaces of the Egyptian pharaohs. He was educated and trained in the way of royalty to be a great leader. He was destined for greatness. You might even say he was highly qualified to be the leader of the children of Israel. We aren't sure at what point Moses discovered that he was of Hebrew birth, nor at what age he sensed God calling him to deliver the children of Israel. But both were present on the day Moses went out to see his people, the children of Israel:

> "One day, when Moses had grown up, he went out to his people and looked on their burdens, and he saw an Egyptian beating a Hebrew, one of his people. He looked this way and that, and seeing no one, he struck down the Egyptian and hid him in the sand.
>
> When he went out the next day, behold, two Hebrews were struggling together. And he said to the man in the wrong, "Why do you strike your companion?"
>
> He answered, "Who made you a prince and a judge over us? Do you mean to kill me as you killed the Egyptian?" Then Moses was afraid, and thought, "Surely the thing is known.'"
> (Exod. 2:11-14)

Moses had a sense of being called by God and wanted to do something, but rather than waiting for God's direction on how to help his people, he took things into his own hands and he killed the abusive Egyptian.

Moses had all the qualifications to be a great leader by earthly standards. He sensed God's calling and did something about it. This is a typical response for us guys, isn't it? We feel a sense of calling; we want to do something; we do it and then wonder, *Oh, shoot. Did I just make that worse?* When God calls us to become something, we often mistakenly step into what we think that means based on our own understanding of what we can and cannot do.

The problem with this line of reasoning is that it doesn't consider God. If you're trying to be a great father by only using your human ability to be great, you will not get far. We hurt the ones we love, even if it's only being so nice, so giving, and not teaching, fathering, about worship, manhood, effort, discipline, love, and forgiveness. This happened to Moses. This is also what happened to a lot of us as we tried to step into becoming what God called us to be based on our own understanding and abilities. Taking matters into our own hands without God's help doesn't work. For God's calling on our lives to be realized, it requires His love, presence, and grace in us and through us. Human zeal and power alone can never accomplish the purposes of God! The Bible says, "Anyone who belongs to Christ has become a new person. The old life is gone; a new life has begun!" (2 Cor. 5:17, NLT).

No matter how qualified you may be, you will not become what God has called you to be in your own strength or ability. To the extent you receive the Father's blessing through His Son, Jesus, into your life, you will become a new person who can fully be the husband and father God has called you to be. The secret to becoming a great man, husband, father, and leader is not your qualification. It is all about receiving God's love, presence, and grace to become what God has called you to be. Think through all the false starts in your life. Did they start with you waiting to receive what you needed from God? I doubt it.

Most, if not all, my false starts, my epic failures, as a parent or husband began when I followed "all about me," just like the Nike slogan Just Do It. How about you?

The opposite of Just Do It is turning your life over, with outstretched arms, to Jesus and being redeemed with His life, hope, vision, and power that come from our Father in heaven. "Receive God's power to do it"—that is the Receiving Principle.

You may have all the qualifications to be a great dad. You may have good experiences from your positive relationship with your father to fall back on. But neither experience nor qualifications will fill you with the power of God to be the great man, husband, and father your family needs.

Experience and qualifications will fall short on their own.

You need to receive the blessing and power of God to become that man, husband, and father that God has called you to be. Can you see that doing something on your own will severely limit the greatness God has called you to?

I'm sure Moses did not understand that the calling he felt to deliver God's people was much bigger than solving one dispute between two Israelites that day. God was calling Moses to set free the entire Israelite nation from the bondage of Egypt! That's not something Moses could have done on his own. He needed to learn how to receive from God to become the man who would become that deliverer.

Peter Receives His Calling

Peter is the disciple who wasn't afraid to say what he was thinking. He had the bad habit of regularly putting his foot in his mouth when he tried to increase himself. Remember when Peter told Jesus he would die for him and Jesus quickly countered, "You will deny me three times"? Peter also had a zealous heart for increasing Jesus. In Matthew 16, Jesus asked His disciples who they thought He was.

> "Simon Peter replied, 'You are the Christ, the Son of the living God.' And Jesus answered him, 'Blessed are you, Simon Bar-Jonah! For flesh and blood has not revealed this to you, but my Father who is in heaven.'" (Matt. 16:16-17)

A few verses later, Peter mistakenly rebuked Jesus, saying:

> "'Far be it from you, Lord! This shall never happen to you.' But he turned and said to Peter, 'Get behind me, Satan! You are a hindrance to me. For you are not setting your mind on the things of God, but on the things of man.'" (Matt. 16:22b-23)

Jesus did not call Peter based on Peter's qualifications as a great leader. God called Peter based on his willingness to follow and receive from Jesus. Peter's heart was open to receiving, and the Father's blessing would fill any lack Peter had to become the leader that God had called him to be. Jesus knew who Peter would become in Him. Is it possible the Father sees you and me in the same way? Absolutely. We are not a great man, husband, or father because of our experience and qualifications. We become a great man, husband, and father according to our willingness to receive from Him.

The Bible says, "But, as it is written, 'What no eye has seen, nor ear heard, nor the heart of man imagined, what God has prepared for those who love him'" (1 Cor. 2:9). The same is true for you and me. We cannot even imagine the blessings the Father has in store for us if we remain open to receiving His help.

In one of Peter's most defining moments, the uneducated fisherman found himself, along with his friends, in the biggest storm he'd ever seen. The Bible says that they were in serious trouble. Jesus had sent His disciples ahead of Him to cross the Sea of Galilee by boat, but at three o'clock in the morning, they were still fighting the waves and getting nowhere. That's when Jesus came walking toward them on the water.

> "When the disciples saw him walking on the water, they were terrified. In their fear, they cried out, 'It's a ghost!' But Jesus spoke to them at once. 'Don't be afraid,' he said. 'Take courage. I am here!'" (Matt. 14:26-27, NLT)

You know when you're looking at huge waves and the horizon keeps appearing and disappearing? I imagine that's why the disciples may have thought Jesus was a ghost—He was walking calmly across the water and kept coming in and out of view as they were tossed around by the waves. It terrified them.

> "Then Peter called to him, 'Lord, if it's really you, tell me to come to you, walking on the water.' 'Yes, come,' Jesus said. So Peter went over the side of the boat and walked on the water toward Jesus.'" (Matt.14:28-29, NLT)

Of all those men on the boat, Peter was the only one brave enough to call out to the ghost. And when Peter heard Jesus invite him out onto the water, he was brave enough to climb over the side of the boat and step out onto the water—into the unknown. Peter was open to receiving the invitation of Jesus as enough to fill him with the ability to walk on water. Peter did not understand what he was doing when he got out of the boat, but he heard Jesus calling him, inviting him, so out of the boat he went.

> "But when he saw the strong wind and the waves, he was terrified and began to sink. 'Save me, Lord!' he shouted. Jesus immediately reached out and grabbed him. 'You have so little faith,' Jesus said. 'Why did you doubt me?' When they climbed back into the boat, the wind stopped. Then the disciples worshiped him. 'You really are the Son of God!' they exclaimed." (Matt. 14:30-33, NLT)

Peter may have had a breakthrough when he stepped out of the boat, but he still had a barrier in his mind. He had a supernatural moment when he walked on the water by keeping his eyes on Jesus. But when he took his eyes off of Jesus and saw the strong wind and the waves, he was terrified and began to sink. The reason he was terrified was because he knew he did not have the ability to walk on water, and he lost faith in Jesus calling him. Like most of us, Peter struggled to receive God's calling when he focused on his abilities rather than on Jesus' abilities. Peter lacked faith and didn't understand that Jesus was the same person who created the universe, including the water. Walking on the water was not a difficult miracle for the Creator of the universe.

The Bible says, "Jesus is the radiance of the glory of God and the exact imprint of his nature, and he upholds the universe by the word of his power" (Heb. 1:3). When the Creator of the universe calls you to become the man, husband, and father your family needs, what do you think is going to happen?

Receiving What God Has Prepared for You

When God called me to plant a church, I had visions of preaching and seeing thousands of people saved every week like I experienced when I preached in Billy Graham's pre-crusades for high schools. I thought I would see the same kind of big ministry when God called me to pastor a local church. After a couple of years we moved our church to the Stadium business park in Anaheim, California, and renamed our church The Stadium Vineyard. It was located right across the street from the Anaheim Stadium. When the Angels baseball team moved from Los Angeles to the Anaheim Stadium, the Southern California Edison company invested in the Stadium rebuilding project and it became known as the "Big Ed." This was an amazing coincidence because I had been known as Big Ed since I was a kid. As soon as the people of our church heard the stadium was called the Big Ed, the church members began asking, "When are we going to move to our new church at the stadium?" Little did I know God was about to teach me something about being Big Ed.

Like Peter, Jesus called me to leave my career as a football player and follow Him into ministry. I quickly discovered that God's call wasn't about my abilities but about Christ's abilities in me. Our church grew quickly to almost 600 and then hit a wall, because, like Peter, I was continuing to look at my ability rather than Jesus' ability in me. After nine months of growth, several people decided to leave and plant their own church. Planting new churches is a wonderful thing, but they planted this church in secret and took almost 100 of our key people without telling us. It devastated me because I didn't see it coming. I had never had people betray me like that. I had been used to the cheering of the crowds and winning as an athlete and as an evangelist. Like Peter, I took my eyes off of Jesus and was looking at the size of the waves and I started sinking. I had lost my focus of Jesus' calling on me and was questioning my ability to pastor the church. Big Ed was not feeling so big.

My best friend, Brian Holloway, invited Jill and me to a getaway in Hawaii with him and his family. I was still reeling from the hurt of our church split and was questioning my calling. Brian hosted Jill and me one night at a beautiful tiki torch lit dinner at a resort on the island of Maui. After finishing an amazing dinner, Brian asked, "How are you doing, brother?" I started telling Brian about the hurtful things I was going through and the mistakes I had made during this time.

After about five minutes, this All-Pro left tackle from the New England Patriots and my best friend from high school looked at me and said, "Are you through?"—like he would say in the locker room at halftime to motivate his team not to quit. "Are you through, Ed Tandy McGlasson?"

I looked at him and asked, "What are you talking about?"

He leaned in and, looking into my eyes, said, "Make me a promise that from this moment on in your life you never tell me that sorry-ass story again! You have lost sight of who God has made you to be. You are making your life about yourself and not about what God wants to teach you. So do me a favor! Stop looking back and start looking at who God is calling you to be."

Jesus spoke to me through Brian's words to turn my eyes from looking at the size of the waves and back to Jesus and His calling on my life. A verse jumped into my heart after Brian spoke to me: "But one thing I do: forgetting what lies behind and straining forward to what lies ahead, I press on toward the goal for the prize of the upward call of God in Christ Jesus" (Phil. 3:13–15).

God was using our church split to teach me that I must let go of the past, which was too much about me, in order to receive my calling for the future. Whether it was my successes as Big Ed or my mistakes and betrayal as a pastor, the truth was that I needed to decrease my focus on myself and increase my focus on Jesus.

This truth is also important in receiving your calling to become the husband and father your family needs. We can only become the man, husband, and father God is calling us to be when we take our eyes off of ourselves and focus them on Jesus.

Think of how Moses and Peter handled their callings from God. Both of them thought they were disqualified through their mistakes, thinking God couldn't use them. We sometimes do that as men, don't we? We easily dismiss ourselves from God's calling on us because we think we don't have what it takes to be the man God is calling us to be.

What we don't understand is that God's calling on us is impossible to do without Him! He isn't calling us because of our capacity to fulfill His calling in our lives. He is calling us based on His capacity in Christ to enable us to fulfill that calling. Deitrich Bonhoeffer wrote, "When Christ calls a man, he bids him come and die." Christ's calling in us to be the husband and father our families need grows to the level that we die to ourselves and lay down our lives so that Christ increases and gets the glory through the things we do in His name.

Remember, He's called you not based on your own abilities but on His capacity to empower you to become the man, husband, and father He's called you to be.

> "A man can receive nothing unless it has been given to him from heaven ... He must increase, but I must decrease." (John 3:27, 30)

Personal Insights

1. Do you believe you can be the husband and father your family needs, even though you have made mistakes?

2. Do you understand that God's calling isn't based on something you already have, but rather on His promises to fill you with His blessing and give you everything you need to answer His call?

3. Are you willing to trust Him and step out of the boat in faith and receive His blessing to be the husband and father He has called you to be?

Key Takeaways

God's plan all along has been to make us into a new kind of man, a whole new version, a powerful version where everything we did before we met Jesus has passed away and no longer has any power over us. Read the words of Paul:

> "From now on, therefore, we regard no one according to the flesh. Even though we once regarded Christ according to the flesh, we regard him thus no longer. Therefore, if anyone is in Christ, he is a new creation. The old has passed away; behold, the new has come." (2 Cor. 5:16–17)

We are not supposed to look at followers of Jesus according to what they do, how much they own, or how much money they have. Godly men are measured by who Christ is in them and how much of His image and blessing of the Father they bear. Nothing is impossible for that kind of man. That is how God sees you when you are in Christ. That is who God has called you to be.

How To's

1.   How do you receive the calling that God has made you for?

The Bible says,

> "… when He who had set me apart before I was born, and who called me by his grace, was pleased to reveal his Son to me, in order that I might preach him among the Gentiles." (Gal. 1:15–16)

God the Father has set all of us apart for a purpose He has called us to. It is the Father's pleasure to reveal His Son to us so that we can fulfill His calling on our lives. Like Paul, when we are able to declare that "God set me apart before

I was born," then that is a powerful moment for us as men. Do you know what God set you apart for? We all need to ask Him what He has called us to become. Then we must quiet ourselves and listen. Rick Warren has advised that we should get alone with God at the end of every year and ask Him to clarify His calling for the next year. Once we know what God is calling us to, we must follow through and do it.

How many of you have been called by God to do something that seemed beyond your ability? When God calls us to do things beyond our human ability, often we stumble and fall short. When we stumble, it's easy to believe the lie that it must be because we can't do it. But falling short of perfection is part of being human. That's why we need to be fathered by God and continuously filled with the Holy Spirit to do the things the Father is calling us to do. You will never be a perfect man, husband, or dad 100 percent of the time. But that doesn't mean you aren't cut out for your calling as a husband or father. It just means that you're human and that you need the Father to give you the grace you need—and what you don't have—to do the job He's called you to do.

**To help you receive the grace you need to be a good father,
we would like to give you a free daily devotional.**
Receive your daily devotional here:
https://www.blessingofthefather.com/free-devotion

2.   How can you see yourself the way the Father sees you?

We must put our faith in Jesus and receive God's mercy and forgiveness. God sees us through the finished work of Jesus. We must fully understand and believe that when the Father looks at us, through Jesus' sacrifice, He sees us as His justified and righteous beloved children. No matter how unqualified we may feel, the Father sees us according to what He can do in us. In His eyes we are His beloved sons and walk with Him just like Jesus did every day.

"Therefore, if anyone is in Christ, he is a new creation. The old
has passed away; behold, the new has come." (2 Cor. 5:17)

If we dwell on our past mistakes, we will be captured by shame. Shame keeps
us from seeing ourselves as God sees us. Shame also keeps us from seeing our
wives and children the way God sees them. Faith in Jesus Christ enables us to see
ourselves and our families the way God sees us. When we see them as God sees
them, we will treat our families the way God treats us. No matter how broken
we feel or our family is, God sees us as a new creation.

3.   How do you receive your calling to become a new person?

There is one thing we must do every day to receive our calling and become the
man, husband, and father that God has called us to be. They are found in Paul's
words:

"But one thing I do: forgetting what lies behind and straining
forward to what lies ahead, I press on toward the goal for the
prize of the upward call of God in Christ Jesus." (Phil. 3:13–15)

We as men tend to hold onto the mistakes of our past. We may have asked
God for forgiveness and received His mercy, but we still live in the regret of our
mistakes. Are you still carrying regret for something you wish you hadn't done
in the past?

Before Paul encountered Jesus, he was called Saul and had a follower of Jesus
named Stephen executed. Stephen was a man "full of grace and power, doing
great wonders and signs among the people" (Acts 6:8). Stephen was an unusu-
ally gifted evangelist of that day. Stephen's last words while being stoned were:

"'Lord Jesus, receive my spirit.' And falling to his knees he cried
out with a loud voice, 'Lord, do not hold this sin against them.'
And when he had said this, he fell asleep. And Saul approved of
his execution." (Acts 7:59–8:1)

Paul not only had to receive forgiveness for what he had done, but he also had to learn to "forget what lies behind" by forgiving himself. Holding onto past mistakes could keep him from receiving God's calling. Living in the regrets of yesterday can keep our hearts from pressing toward the "prize of the upward call of God in Christ Jesus." It's our pride and shame that keep us holding onto our past, because we are still trying to analyze why we fell short so we can fix ourselves. Because of that behavior, we haven't fully received God's forgiveness. It is our faith that Jesus' sacrifice paid for all of our sins that allows us to receive God's forgiveness. Not believing that God's forgiveness is big enough to cover our sins is a bad place to be. When we withhold forgiveness for ourselves, we are saying that Christ's sacrifice wasn't enough to cover us. When we learn to forgive ourselves the same way Christ has forgiven us, it sets us free from the mistakes of our past. I think Stephen's last words, "Lord, do not hold this sin against them," likely haunted Paul until he learned to receive God's mercy and forgiveness.

Here are two things that we can do to receive His forgiveness and become the new man God called us to be:

1.   Write down anything you need to forget that you are still holding onto.

2.   Forgive yourself by praying, "Father, forgive me for holding onto the things that You have already forgiven. I choose to forgive myself right now for [name those things out loud] in the name of Jesus. Father, give me the courage to let go of my past and press toward the goal of my calling in You. Jesus, I receive my calling of becoming the man, husband, and father You have created me to be. In Jesus' name. Amen!

Do you have a friend who needs a new beginning with his family?
Click here to send him a copy of this book
and use the code "newbeginning" for a 10% discount.
https://www.blessingofthefather.com/howtobecome

Prayer

Father, give me the courage to let go of my past and press toward the goal of my calling in You. Jesus, I receive my calling of becoming the man, husband, and father You have created me to be. In Jesus' name. Amen!

CHAPTER 3

RECEIVING: IN THE WILDERNESS

Where shall I go from your Spirit? Or where shall I flee from your presence? If I ascend to heaven, you are there! If I make my bed in Sheol, you are there!

Psalm 139:7–8

Running into the Wilderness

When I used the total of my NFL earnings to buy a lobster-fishing boat and all the equipment with no experience, my wife, Jill, came to the dock with our son Edward to see me off. She said, "Ed, I pray God doesn't kill you for being so dumb." I laugh every time I think about that story now. I didn't like it when she said it, but she was right! God called me into the ministry, but I didn't have the first clue about what that meant. He was calling me into a level of trust in my relationship with Him I hadn't experienced before.

Scared and unsure of what my future was, I set off in my lobster-fishing boat for Catalina Island, an island local to our coast here in Southern California. You might say I was running away, but I honestly thought I was doing something productive with my life. I sure am glad God doesn't kill people for being dumb!

My career as a lobster fisherman was cut short by an extreme storm that decimated the lobster-fishing industry that year. I nearly died on Catalina Island and came home with a renewed trust and willingness to follow God's plan instead of my own.

No one likes to talk about running away, least of all us men. We aren't running away; we're spending all this time on our hobbies to relax! We aren't avoiding God's calling on our lives; we're just too busy working to provide for our families! Have you been there too? Our pride often impedes us hearing our wives' wisdom when they say things like, "I pray God doesn't kill you for being so dumb." Thank God for praying mothers and wives! I knew God was calling me to something beyond the NFL and way beyond my ability. That initial nudge from the Holy Spirit left me both excited and fearful. I was excited by a new direction and fearful of the unknown. What should I do now? How will I provide for my family? Who would want to listen to a football player preach?

God's calling is always beyond what we can do in our own strength, and that is scary. Why is that so hard for us? Because we like to be in control of our future. We want to create a future where we are the heroes of our stories and project that image to others. When Adam, our greatest of grandfathers, sinned against God, it was because he wanted to be the hero of his story without God. The temptation is the same for each of us today. Our most significant places of failure and brokenness come when we try to live our life without God, or when we try to live out His calling in our own strength. It takes both humility and trust to follow God into the adventure He is calling us to.

It's okay to feel afraid or inadequate. God has grace for that, too. He's the God of second, third, and fourth chances! When I returned from my boating experience, God spoke to me again: "In that day the Lord will extend his hand yet a second time to recover the remnant that remains of his people … from the coastlands of the sea" (Isaiah 11:11). I didn't realize that no matter where you run to—or boat to—God is already there. He is the God of second chances!

After Moses tried to be a deliverer in his own strength and killed the Egyptian, he was afraid. The Bible says, "When Pharaoh heard of it, he sought to kill

Moses. But Moses fled from Pharaoh and stayed in the land of Midian. And he sat down by a well" (Exod. 2:15). He had a sense of calling at the moment he tried to defend his Israelite brother from the Egyptian beating him, but later he was only left with fear. And he ran. Have you been there? Have you felt a sense of God's calling in one moment, destined for greatness, only to be pursued by an overwhelming sense of fear and apprehension? You are not alone.

Moses ran to the wilderness and found a family there. He met the priest of Midian and married one of his seven daughters, Zipporah, and lived in the desert as a shepherd, husband, and later as a father, for forty years. We have no record of what Moses thought about his calling as Israel's deliverer. Did he doubt that God had called him? Probably. Did he think it was all over for him? Probably. Did he believe that he had ruined everything? Probably. I'm sure Moses had little hope that he would ever return to his homeland again.

The wilderness is a place we all go to. It's when we realize that on our own, we'll often blow it. We don't have what it takes to be a great man, husband, or father without God's help. We want to be, sure! But when it comes down to it, we fall short. When we fall short, it often sends us running toward the wilderness. The wilderness isn't always a bad thing. It's a place of testing. The problem is that many of us stay there. We think there isn't hope for us or that we're too flawed to go back. But it's not true. Men have been running to the wilderness, scared of who they are or what they've done, for years. We aren't the only ones who have blown it.

> "One day while Moses was out tending his father-in-law's sheep, he saw a bush enveloped in flames and yet not consumed. And Moses said, 'I will turn aside to see this great sight, why the bush is not burned.' When the Lord saw that he turned aside to see, God called to him out of the bush, 'Moses, Moses!' And he said, 'Here I am.'" (Exod. 3:3-4)

God didn't just shout out at Moses, "Hey! I'm over here!" God waited until

Moses turned aside and was ready to receive. What is it that moves our hearts to that place where we receive from God? The wilderness is a place that God uses to prepare us to receive from Him. Once we are humble and prepared to receive, He reveals Himself and saves us.

> "When we were utterly helpless, Christ came at just the right time and died for us sinners." (Rom. 5:6, NLT)

God has always been the one who's taken the first step to reveal Himself to us. Remember, "For God so loved the world he gave us his only son, that whoever believes in Him would not perish but have everlasting life" (John 3:16).

Peter Receives in the Wilderness

Peter went from anonymity as a fisherman to being an apostle and leader of Jesus' church. But on the night before Jesus' crucifixion, Peter denied that he knew Jesus—not once, not twice, but three times. Peter did this even after Jesus foretold that he would, and even after Jesus prayed for him. After Jesus was arrested, the Bible says that Peter was warming himself over a charcoal fire when he was accused three times of being a follower of Jesus Christ. Peter denied Jesus each time. "And immediately the rooster crowed a second time. And Peter remembered how Jesus had said to him, 'Before the rooster crows twice, you will deny me three times.' And he broke down and wept bitterly" (Mark 14:72).

Peter must have been so ashamed and disgusted with himself. I've been in the wilderness of disgust too many times to count. Sometimes the wilderness looks like a place of shame rooted deep within our hearts because we did the very thing we promised we would never do.

Did you know that Jesus went into the wilderness, too? He had been fasting in the desert forty days when "the tempter came and said to him, 'If you are the Son of God, command these stones to become loaves of bread'" (Matt. 4:3).

The purpose of the devil's attack was to challenge Jesus' identity—His Sonship in His Father. The devil was saying, "If you are the Son of God, then prove it." Jesus could say no to the temptations because He knew who He was, a beloved Son, and was so connected to the love and presence of His Father.

When we're in the wilderness, the devil also seeks to undermine our identity, our adoption as beloved sons and daughters of the Father. When we are unclear about who we are, we are more easily tempted and named by the sin the devil tempts us with. He wants to keep us from our inheritance as children of God by causing us to name ourselves by our brokenness, or sin. He tries to get us to be ashamed and to believe that we have to prove ourselves to God before He will love and bless us. But that is not true! Here's God's promise to us:

> "Look upon my enemies, for they are many, and they hate me with violent hatred. Guard my soul and deliver me; Do not let me be ashamed for I take refuge in you." (Psalm 25:19-20, NASB)

When shame causes us to run to the wilderness and attempt to solve our problems on our own, we are playing into the devil's hand. But when we turn our problems over to God and "take refuge" in the Father's love and mercy, He will not allow shame to rule us.

Peter thought his own boldness and courage would equip him to be faithful to Jesus, but Peter failed just like we all do when we try to battle the devil's temptations in our own strength. The devil loves it when we man up and try to take him on our own. After Peter's denial, I imagine that he questioned whether he was a follower of Jesus at all? Hadn't Judas just betrayed Jesus as well? He probably wondered, *Does that make me like Judas? I know Jesus prayed for me. I know He loves me. But could He forgive this betrayal? I'm just a fisherman. Why would Jesus want me after I failed Him in His greatest hour of need?* Can you hear the devil's accusations in those words as he tried to label Peter with shame?

Jesus later restored Peter over a charcoal fire—one of only two charcoal fires mentioned in the entire Bible. The first charcoal fire mentioned was the moment when Peter denied Jesus, and the second was when Jesus restored Peter during breakfast. This breakfast was a defining moment for Peter. It was a moment when Peter received the love and mercy of his heavenly Father modeled by Jesus. Peter, overwhelmed by shame and no doubt feeling like a failure, tried to run away from God's call on his life by going back to fishing. He probably believed that his denial of Jesus would forever disqualify him from his new identity as a fisher of men and from being close to Jesus again. But it wasn't true.

When we become ashamed and feel unworthy of who God has called us to be, we may go back to our old identity. In Peter's case he went back to what he knew, fishing. In our case it might be our job, a hobby we love, or our addictions. We see ourselves through our failure by naming ourselves by our brokenness. We connect our identity with our biggest mistakes. For example, "My name is Peter. I'm the guy who denied Jesus three times in his hour of need." Or it might be, "I'm Jim and I'm divorced," or "I'm Bob and I'm an addict," or "I'm Steve and I'm a bad father." That's the place of wilderness for men—where we run away from God's presence because we think we are unworthy. But our Father sees us through the sacrifice of Christ and loves us enough to help us overcome any problem, including shame.

> "No, in all these things we are more than conquerors through him who loved us. For I am sure that neither death nor life, nor angels nor rulers, nor things present nor things to come, nor powers, nor height nor depth, nor anything else in all creation, will be able to separate us from the love of God in Christ Jesus our Lord." (Rom. 8:37–39)

The wilderness is a place where God meets us to teach us about who He is. It is not a place of great provision; it is a place where God pursues you to reveal that He is your loving Father so that you can become the man He has called you to be. In the wilderness you learn how to receive and trust the Lord for more. Moses and Peter came to a place where they ran out of their ability to do what God had called them to do and God's love restored them. The wilderness is a place where

God turns us into the sons He has called us to become. Like Moses encountering God at the burning bush, or Peter coming face to face with Jesus at breakfast after he denied Him, when they encountered and received the love and mercy of God for themselves, their stories changed forever. The same is true for you and me.

God Speaks in the Wilderness

Ten years ago I met a man named Joe after one of our Sunday church services. He came up to me to tell me his story:

> "I had been arrested and was waiting to be sentenced with eleven other men who were a part of the Mexican mafia. The day before I was supposed to go in front of the judge, I walked by a cell where there was an inmate who was one of those people in prison we called 'the man.' Nobody messed with him, or he messed with you. He was living out his own life sentence.
>
> I noticed an open Bible on his top bunk and stopped and asked, 'What's this?'
>
> He said, 'It's a Bible. Do you have a problem with that?' He looked at me dead in the eye.
>
> 'No, no disrespect,' I replied. 'Can I ask you why you have it?'
>
> 'I read it so I can hear God's voice. I have become a follower of Jesus,' the man responded.
>
> 'You?' I asked.
>
> 'Yes and I read this book and God speaks to me.'
>
> 'He does? He has never spoken to me. How can I hear God speak to me?' I asked.
>
> 'All you gotta do, Joe, is pray to God and ask Him for anything and He will give it to you,' he said.
>
> 'Really! Anything?' I asked with a puzzled look.
>
> 'Really. All you gotta do is go down to your cell and ask God for anything and He'll give it to you.'

So I prayed, 'God, if You are real, I am asking You that when I come before the judge for my sentencing, he gives me 'time served' for my sentence so I can get out of prison. I know I deserve more time, but I am asking You to do that for me, and if You do this, I'll give You the rest of my life!'

The next morning I came up before the judge after two of my other co-conspirators. The first one was given a life sentence and the second got twenty years for being leaders of the Mexican mafia. I was expecting the judge to throw the book at me but I heard him say, 'I don't think prison is a place you're supposed to be, so I'm going to give you credit for your time served and set you free.'

I yelled out, 'Time served? For real, judge?' I couldn't believe what I had just heard and how God had answered my prayer.

'Yes!' the judge replied.

When I was released, I got in my car and started driving around, wondering how I could give my life to Jesus to fulfill the promise I made to God if I got out of jail. I prayed, 'Okay, I need You in my life but I don't know how to give my life to You. Where do I go?'

At that moment I was driving on the 55 freeway in Southern California and I saw your church sign that says 'Want Jesus? Turn left here.' So I pulled into the church parking lot and walked through the front door. Not seeing anybody around, I yelled out, 'Is there anybody here?'

'Yes! I am here,' Associate Pastor Glen answered. He came out of his upstairs office and asked, 'How can I help you?'

I said, 'I'm here because I want to give my life to Jesus and I don't know how to do it.'

Pastor Glen replied, 'Come on up, and I will show you how to ask Jesus into your life: "If you confess with your mouth that

Jesus is Lord and believe in your heart that God raised him from the dead, you will be saved. For with the heart one believes and is justified, and with the mouth one confesses and is saved."" (Rom. 10:9–11)

Joe prayed with Glen that night and gave his life to Jesus. Joe is living proof that you're only a prayer away from the love and mercy of God and a new beginning. All you have to do is ask God for His mercy and receive it. Joe left that jail cell as an ex-con and became the father to his children that he never experienced with his dad. If you ever wondered if God can change your story too, remember Joe's story and ask God for the miracle you need. His promises and voice are just a prayer away. He is a good, good Father.

God's Power in the Wilderness

You cannot be the father your kids need you to be, the husband your wife needs you to be, and the man God has called you to be without the empowering of the Holy Spirit. You might have a good run, but you will never fully realize God's calling for your life and cross the finish line on your own without the empowering presence of the Holy Spirit.

"But if the Spirit of Him who raised Jesus from the dead dwells in you, He who raised Jesus from the dead will also give life to your mortal bodies through His Spirit who dwells in you." (Rom. 8:11)

So how do we receive God's Holy Spirit? We find the secret in this verse:

"And I tell you, ask, and it will be given to you; seek, and you will find; knock, and it will be opened to you.... If you then, who are evil, know how to give good gifts to your children, how much

more will the heavenly Father give the Holy Spirit to those who
ask him!" (Luke 11:9–13)

When you ask the Holy Spirit to come into your life, Jesus promises us that
He will. When God the Father gave His Son, Jesus, to die in our place, all the sin
and punishment we deserved was placed upon Jesus as He hung on the cross.
There is nothing we can do against God that Jesus hasn't already paid the price
for. That's why we can ask the Holy Spirit to come into our lives and help us
overcome any obstacle, including shame.

Moving into the place of receiving happens when we approach the Father
and ask Him for His Holy Spirit to help us connect to His steadfast love and
mercy. We learn in those moments where the power to help us comes from:
His Holy Spirit.

"If God is for us, who is against us? He who did not spare His
own Son, but delivered Him over for us all, how will He not
give us all things?" (Rom. 8:31-32)

God loves using the wilderness to show us who He is so that we can become
everything He has called us to be. Are you ready to receive? Are you ready to be
restored by the love of the Father? If the answer to those questions is yes, then
get ready for the most incredible transformation of your life.

Personal Insights

1. Have you run away from things God has called you to do?

2. What did you run away from?

3. Can you fulfill your calling as a husband and father without God's help?

4. How often have you asked God to send His Holy Spirit to help you?

Key Takeaways

In order to receive in the wilderness, you need the Holy Spirit. You cannot be the father your kids need you to be, the husband your wife needs you to be, and the man God has called you to be without the empowering of the Holy Spirit. You might have a good run, but you will never fully realize God's calling for your life and cross the finish line on your own without the empowering presence of the Holy Spirit.

> "But if the Spirit of Him who raised Jesus from the dead dwells
> in you, He who raised Jesus from the dead will also give life
> to your mortal bodies through His Spirit who dwells in you."
> (Rom. 8:11)

Here is an amazing promise in the verse for us: Because we have the person of the Holy Spirit dwelling in us, there is nothing He can't heal in our life or the lives of our families.

How To's

1. How do you stop running away from the things God is calling you to do?

To stop running away we have to trust God instead of our own ability. Men hate to admit it, but we can't fix everything by ourselves. We cannot respond to God's calling in our own ability. Sometimes when life becomes tough and we are unable to solve the problem, we run. We don't like to admit we are running or hiding. We use the excuse of our job being too demanding, or we immerse ourselves in our hobbies or our addictions.

Fear begins when we look at our own capacity to do what God has asked us to do and we don't feel like we can do it. A simple example is when God is calling us to humble ourselves to ask our wife or children to forgive us. We tell ourselves we don't want to do it, but really we are afraid of being vulnerable. So we run from it by putting it off or avoiding the conversation, or we may get angry and shout it away, just like our dads did. Some of us run to alcohol or other addictions.

Where does the fear come from? It comes because we don't know how to fix it ourselves. Our cups are empty because our own fathers did not know how to be vulnerable with us. We have a hard time believing that God has our back when we step out in faith, because, like our fathers, we believe we have to do it in our own ability. To stop running we must trust in God's capacity to empower us to do those things that we can't do on our own.

**To access God's power every day,
we recommend reading our daily devotional.**

Access our free daily devotional here:
https://www.blessingofthefather.com/daily-devotional

2.   How do you receive in the wilderness?

Feed your faith and starve your fear. Fix your attention on God and learn how to think like God thinks by filling your mind and your heart with God's Word.

> "Don't become so well-adjusted to your culture that you fit into it without even thinking. Instead, fix your attention on God. You'll be changed from the inside out. Readily recognize what he wants from you and quickly respond to it. Unlike the culture around you, always dragging you down to its level of immaturity, God brings the best out of you, develops well-formed maturity in you." (Rom. 12:2, MSG)

Ask and believe. You need to ask God for help and believe that when you ask God for help, He gives it to you.

> "And Jesus answered them, 'Have faith in God. Truly, I say to you, whoever says to this mountain, Be taken up and thrown into the sea,' and does not doubt in his heart, but believes that what he says will come to pass, it will be done for him. Therefore, I tell you, whatever you ask in prayer, believe that you have received it, and it will be yours.'" (Mark 11:22–24)

Prayer

Father, open my ears to Your calling on my life and give me the courage to follow You wherever You go. Forgive me for trying to live my life in my own strength. If Your presence doesn't go with me, I won't go. Without You I don't have a calling, so I am done running away from You. Thank You for using the wilderness in my life and showing me that I can trust You and follow You. I am Your servant. Use me any way You want. In Jesus' name! Amen.

CHAPTER 4

RECEIVING: OUR ADOPTION

Long before he laid down earth's foundations, he had us in mind,
had settled on us as the focus of his love, to be made whole and
holy by his love. Long, long ago he decided to adopt us into his
family through Jesus Christ.
(What pleasure he took in planning this!)

Ephesians 1:3–5, MSG

God planned to adopt you into His family before He made the heavens and earth. Before Adam and Eve sinned and fell, God made a plan to restore His sons and daughters to Himself through adoption. When Jesus died on the cross in the place of you and me, He paid the price for our sin and prepared the way for our adoption by God.

Introducing—God the Father

The Old Testament is filled with scriptures about who God is. But the Old Testament depicts God's relationship with fallen man and fallen creation. Many have read sections of the Old Testament and come away thinking God was angry. They don't understand that God is holy and that to have a relationship with Him, you must be holy too. The Father made us to have an unending relationship with Him. It was the sin and rebellion of mankind that separated us from the love and presence of God. His plan all along was to be our Father.

> "I will be a father to you, and you shall be sons and daughters to me, says the Lord Almighty." (2 Cor. 6:18)

When Jesus arrived on the scene talking about God as a Father, this was a new revelation. No one had ever talked about God as a Father before. Jesus spoke about the Father as though they had a close, intimate relationship.

> "So Jesus explained himself at length. 'I'm telling you this straight. The Son can't independently do a thing, only what he sees the Father doing. What the Father does, the Son does. The Father loves the Son and includes him in everything he is doing.'" (John 5:19, MSG)

This was almost impossible for those listening at the time to imagine. I'm sure they were thinking, *So, You're saying that Go*, *the same holy Go*, *that le*, *us out of Egypt, tells You everything He* *oes an*, *loves You like a Son?* They couldn't fathom it. Moses had a closeness with God that they recognized, but that was Moses. Jesus calling God His Father was beyond their imaginations.

The children of Israel did not view God as their Father. Their relationship with Him, aside from a select few men of great faith, was formal, and perhaps distant. God as their Father was as strange to them as it may feel for some of you. And also, Jesus claimed that this idea of God as their Father was not something new. God had always wanted to be their Father. He had always wanted to have a close, intimate relationship with each of His children.

Jesus lived a joy-filled "like Father, like Son" relationship with His Father that the Jewish religious leaders did not understand. The Bible says of Jesus,

"You have loved righteousness and hated wickedness; therefore
God, your God, has anointed you with the oil of gladness beyond
your companions." (Heb. 1:9)

He had a "like Father, like Son" relationship with God because He had no
sin to separate Him from the Father. His relationship with the Father—leading
Him, calling Him, sharing with Him what He was doing—is the same relationship God the Father wants to have with you. Jesus died for you and me on the
cross so that in Him we can have the same unrestricted "like Father, like son"
relationship Jesus had.

"Therefore, since we have been justified by faith, we have peace
with God through our Lord Jesus Christ. Through him we have
also obtained access by faith into this grace in which we stand,
and we rejoice in hope of the glory of God." (Rom. 5:1-2)

The Greek word for "justified" means "to declare, pronounce, to be just, and
righteous." When Jesus took our sins upon Himself on the cross, He made us
right with God, as we were created to be. Jesus opened the door to the Father's
house. We can now have the same "like Father, like son" relationship with God
that Jesus has.

When we receive our adoption from God the Father, we can become just
like Him. The more we become like Jesus and the Father, the more blessings we
have to give our kids. It is the person we become that frames the future stories
of our kids and grandkids.

I saw this in the way God fathered His Son, Jesus. Jesus was the perfect repre-
sentation and image of the Father. Jesus Himself said, "Whoever has seen me
has seen the Father" (John 14:9). That became my new goal as a dad. I wanted to
become like Jesus and the Father. I wanted to be fathered by God the same way
Jesus was so that I could father my children the same way.

No Longer Slaves but Sons

What needs to happen for us to enter this "like Father, like son" relationship that Jesus had with the Father? The first step is learning to receive our adoption as sons. So many men I know consider their relationship with God more as rules and regulations they need to follow to be blessed. That is religion, not a relationship. Following the rules of the family doesn't make you an adopted member of the family, just like your kids following the rules of your home isn't what makes them your kids. There is something more to your relationship than that.

There is a moment when we are born again into His family (salvation) and when we are adopted as His sons (the blessing of the Father). God sent His Son, Jesus, to redeem us so that we might receive adoption as sons. And because you are sons, God has sent the Spirit of his Son into our hearts, crying, "'Abba! Father!' So you are no longer a slave, but a son, and if a son, then an heir through God" (Gal. 4:5b-7).

Although the receiving of our inheritance as sons of God seems like a simple act, it is a step many Christians have not taken. They have believed in Jesus for their salvation to go to heaven, but they haven't received their adoption as sons and daughters. They are still acting like they are the slaves or servants in the household. Imagine a servant in the household of God. They would be blessed to work there, wouldn't they? Like the psalmist who said, "I would rather be a doorkeeper in the house of my God than dwell in the tents of wickedness" (Ps. 84:10b).

Except the difference is, you're walking around the Father's house, the King's house, acting like you're so blessed to be a servant when you're really a son! You're the prince, not a slave! How crazy is that? And yet, some of us are living our lives just like that. We are a son in the Father's house, yet we're living like one of the hired servants.

The Father wants us to step into our rightful place as His adopted sons and daughters, the position redeemed for us by the precious blood of His Son, Jesus. In receiving this gift of adoption and God's Holy Spirit, we become a son, with all the wisdom, grace, and power needed to be the man, husband, and father God created us to be. Paul wrote more about our new relationship with God as our Father, saying,

> "This resurrection life you received from God is not a timid, grave-tending life. It's adventurously expectant, greeting God with a childlike 'What's next, Papa?' God's Spirit touches our spirits and confirms who we really are. We know who he is, and we know who we are: Father and children. And we know we are going to get what's coming to us—an unbelievable inheritance! We go through exactly what Christ goes through. If we go through the hard times with him, then we're certainly going to go through the good times with him!" (Rom. 8:15-17, MSG)

Free from Our Father's Prison

Some friends of mine invited me to speak in a Missouri maximum-security prison about Jesus and the blessing of the Father. The guards escorted me through security to a makeshift stage area inside the main cell block. They ushered in the prisoners to sit in bleachers. I watched as the inmates walked in and sat with their groups. The last guy who walked in got a bunch of nods from the other prisoners as he sat down. He appeared to be notorious with the group, but I didn't know why. As I watched him, the Lord opened up my heart. I didn't see a prisoner or a thug; I saw a boy who had never known a father's love, a boy who, I discovered after the event, had followed his own father's footsteps into a life of crime—convicted of the same crime his father was: murder! As the worship team played, I stepped down from the stage and sat down next to this man to the dismay of the guards.

As I sat down, the man asked me, "What are you doing here?"

I looked at him and said, "God sent me here today for you." He asked who I was, so I responded, "I'm Ed. Who are you?"

He kept silent, puzzled by my total disregard for his infamous position in prison. As the worship team was singing their last song, I got up to return to the stage. The man asked, "What do you want? Everybody wants something."

I smiled and said, "Just listen today. Jesus will speak to you."

Back on stage, I shared the message God had put on my heart for these men. About halfway through the message I said, "Many of you in this room had fathers who imprisoned you by their own brokenness. The lack of a father's love has put you in this prison. God sent me here today to set you free from the prison your fathers built." Within a few moments, the notorious leader stood to his feet and walked forward. He was doing everything he could do to keep from crying. He raised his arms and cried out to Jesus to heal his life. Men began clearing the bleachers, coming forward to receive Jesus. Over four hundred men raised their hands to receive Jesus that day.

As the men were standing there, I asked how many of them had not been a good father to their children. Every hand went up. As I prayed for them to receive the blessing their own fathers never gave them, there wasn't a dry eye in the room—mine included. I remember looking down and seeing the man I had spoken to—the boy who had never known a father's love—experiencing the love of Jesus. He pointed to me, and with tears in his eyes, he smiled. It was a smile that said, "I will never be the same. I will set my children free from the prison I have built for them."

You don't have to be a convicted criminal to be imprisoned by the wounds of your father. Do you still feel you are stuck in the prison of your father?

My best friend in heaven, James Ryle, was born to a father who ended up getting in trouble and spending time in prison. James, after being sent to an orphanage with his five brothers and sisters, ended up in prison just like his dad. James had a dramatic encounter with the Lord in prison and felt like he was supposed to find his dad, whom he hadn't seen in over twenty years. Here is part of his conversation from his book *Released from the Prison My Father Built*:

"Dad, which prison were you in?"

"I was in the Coffield Unit," he replied, unaware of all that was lingering behind my question. The moment I heard his answer, my countenance dropped. It was not the same prison unit I had been in. I had thought for sure it was going to be the same and had envisioned preaching rousing sermons about being in the same prison that your father was in; you know, the old "like father, like son" thing. But none of this mattered now. His answer changed all that.

"Which prison were you in?" he then asked me, not knowing how my mind was racing. Somewhat dejected, I replied, "I was in the Ferguson Unit, near Midway, Texas; just down the road from Huntsville."

My dad's expression changed immediately. He went from being curious, to being stunned. His mouth dropped open, and he looked at me in disbelief. Gathering himself, he then said the words that would forever mark my life.

"Dear God, son, I built that prison."

"What?" I replied, "What do you mean, you built it?"

"They used prison labor to build the Ferguson Unit," Dad answered. "I was the welder on the work crew. I welded the bars when that prison was built."

How many of you feel imprisoned by the wounds from your dad?

James's story didn't end there.

As Dad's words hung there in the air, the Lord Jesus spoke to my heart, "James, I have set you free from a prison your father built. Now I will use you to set others free from prisons their fathers have built. Go home to your friends and tell them what great things I have done."[1]

---

1   James Ryle, *Release• from the Prison My Father Built* (Truth Works), pp. 21-22.

That is the picture of what God the Father wants to do for every one of us. The wound that has imprisoned so many sons and daughters will be the very thing that God will use to build His family again when He turns the hearts of fathers back to their children. It is a staggering truth that the way we love our kids will either build the prison from our father wounds or set them free into the adventure that God has designed for them.

There is only one antidote to the father wounds in our story. We need an encounter with a new Father. We need the blessing that lives in the heart of our heavenly Father. The dream He has for each one of us is that we would be like His Son and experience the same love that defined the Father/Son relationship of God with Jesus. Nothing short of that will do.

Jesus prayed for us:

> "I made known to them your name, and I will continue to make it known, that the love with which you have loved me may be in them, and I in them." (John 17:26)

What was the name He made known to them? "Father."

Receiving His Grace

When you think of the word "grace," how would you define it? My best friend in heaven, James Ryle, said, "Grace is the empowering presence of God that enables you to do what He has called you to and become who He has called you to be." I love that! To receive God's grace as sons, we need to believe that God is who He says He is and that we are the sons He says we are—just like Jesus did.

When Jesus fed the crowd of four thousand people, He first asked His disciples, "'How many loaves do you have?' They said, 'Seven'" (Mark 8:5). The disciples were looking at the provisions they had, not the grace Jesus promised them. The number of people could have easily been over eight thousand or more with women and children. Left to their own capabilities, they surveyed the situation in the same ways we would—by our own human capacity or ability. They didn't understand who their Father in heaven was yet. They were thinking, *Well, based on the fact that there are approximately eight thousand people here, and considering we are in the middle of nowhere, and bearing in mind that not even one month's wages would cover the cost of the food, assuming there was somewhere nearby to purchase that amount of food, it's impossible.* But God the Father's grace was there waiting for them to take a step and receive it.

> "And he directed the crowd to sit down on the ground. And he
> took the seven loaves, and having given thanks, he broke them
> and gave them to his disciples to set before the people; and they
> set them before the crowd." (Mark 8:6)

The disciples didn't have the grace or the faith to feed those people until they picked up the baskets in response to Jesus' request and started handing out the food. And consider with me for a moment how it would have even been possible for them to carry baskets full of enough food for all those people. The baskets would have broken. And even if the baskets hadn't broken, the disciples would not have had the physical strength to carry around and distribute that much food. That tells me that the baskets of food were refilling supernaturally as the disciples carried them to the people to feed them. I can imagine the look on their faces when Jesus said, "You feed them." *You have got to be kidding me!* Those looks changed when the baskets they were holding refilled supernaturally every time someone grabbed a piece of bread or fish.

That's the way it works in God's kingdom. His provision is connected to our willingness to step out in faith and trust Him as a Father and receive His adoption. The Father loves to turn the little we have in our baskets into a feast that can feed thousands. Jesus wants all of us to understand that God is a good, good Father who loves to answer our prayers when we ask as a son.

Receiving for Our Children

What does receiving our adoption have to do with becoming better husbands and fathers? Everything.

When we submit and surrender to God's authority and receive His blessing as an adopted son, it changes the way we father our kids. Remember, it is the man we become in Christ that creates a path for our kids to know the way to the Father and His Son. Our job as fathers is to be the person we want our children to become. Being a good father is less about the rules and more about the relationship of love we build with our kids. They know we aren't perfect. They are constantly watching how we navigate the life God has given us. As we follow Christ as a beloved son, we are creating a living playbook for them to follow.

To be a good father, we need to build the same "like Father, like son" relationship with our kids that God the Father had with His Son, Jesus. What made Jesus so irresistible was His loving relationship with His Father. Jesus found pleasure in the Father, and the Father found pleasure in Him. The pleasure, favor, and power of the Father were clear in everything Jesus did. When our kids see in us the same "like Father, like son" relationship Jesus had, they will find it irresistible.

Knowing who we are in Christ and knowing who our kids are in Christ, the dearly beloved sons and daughters of God, is really important. When we begin to understand that God not only wants to Father us but also our children, it changes the way we father. I began to realize that my job as a father was to prepare my children to receive their own adoption as beloved sons and daughters of the Father. My job wasn't to be a perfect dad but to father them the same way I was being fathered by God. The day your children receive their adoption is a great day, because you realize that long after you're gone they will have God to Father them and your grandchildren too. That is the ultimate legacy.

When I received my own adoption as a son, He began to open my heart to who He made me to be. Knowing who I was, a beloved son of God, empowered me to begin fathering my children for their sake and not mine. When a father is not sure about his own identity, it is easy for him to use his children to prove his worth in the world. You see that on every little league field, as some fathers push their kids to perform so they can have bragging rights in the stands.

Knowing you're a son is a powerful place for a man. Most men I meet feel alone in their story, because although their father might have been around when they were kids, he wasn't present. He wasn't available to them because he was trying to figure out his own story. That kind of father wound pushes boys to do everything they can just to be seen. Sadly, as those boys become men, their father wound of desiring to be seen looks like what our culture now calls "toxic masculinity," which further isolates these men from the world. The only way to heal these father wounds is to be fathered by God.

Personal Insights

Take some time to think through following questions and jot down your answers.

1.   Are you still living in the prison your father built?
2.   In what ways are your children living in the prison you have built?
3.   How can you receive the blessing of the Father so you can walk out of the prison your father built?
4.   How can you help your children walk out of the prison you have built?

Key Takeaways

Many of us are still living in the prison our fathers built without even realizing it. How many of us have said we wouldn't do the same things to our children our fathers did to us and yet we have done the same things. When we come to know God as our Father and receive His adoption as sons and daughters, we can walk out of our fathers' prisons and into the love and blessing of a perfect Father:

"…and I will be a father to you, and you shall be sons and daughters to me, says the Lord Almighty." (2 Cor. 6:18)

As a son like Jesus, you have access to everything Jesus had access to. Once we become sons like Jesus was, we are given the grace to become the husband and father our families need.

How To's

1. How do you leave behind the prison your father built?

You can leave the prison your father built the moment you understand and receive that God the Father created you to be loved and adopted by Him. And when you receive your adoption as a son, you will no longer be a prisoner in the cell that your father built.

"So you are no longer a slave, but a son, and if a son, then an heir through God." (Gal. 4:7)

There is only one antidote to the false names and father wounds in our story. We need an encounter with a new Father. We need the blessing that lives in the heart of our heavenly Father. The dream He has for each of us is that we would be like His Son and experience the same love that defined the Father/Son relationship of God the Father and His Son, Jesus. Nothing short of that will do. How will the Father do that for us? Jesus prayed,

"I made known to them your name, and I will continue to make it known, that the love with which you have loved me may be in them, and I in them." (John 17:26)

What was the name He made known to them? "Father."

2. How do you receive for your children?

Receiving for your children is all about you being fathered by God the same way Jesus was. Remember, it is the man you become in Christ that creates a path for your kids to know the way to the Father and His Son. Our job as fathers is to be the person we want our kids to be.

Receiving from the Father every day by spending time with Him reading His Word and praying equips you as a man, husband, and father more than any other activity in your life. The more time you give to being fathered by God, the better father you will be to your kids.

**To help you receive from the Father everyday
signup for a free daily devotional!**
https://www.blessingofthefather.com/daily-devotional

Prayer

Father, thank You for providing me with everything I need in Your Son, Jesus. Thank You for saving me and forgiving my sins. Thank You for making me a part of Your family. Father, I receive my adoption as a beloved son, and I declare that I am no longer limited by the sins of my past or the prison my father built. I am forgiven by Your mercy, saved by Your grace, born again by Your Holy Spirit, and adopted as Your beloved son. I receive my inheritance as a son in Christ and every spiritual blessing I need to live my life for Your glory and to become the husband and father my family needs. In Jesus' name, amen!

CHAPTER 5

RECEIVING: WHILE LEADING

For everyone who asks receives, and the one who seeks finds, and
to the one who knocks it will be opened.

Luke 11:9

We have to ask first, but we also have to learn how to receive. In order to receive, we have to believe that God is a good father and wants to bless us.

> "And Jesus answered them, 'Have faith in God. Truly, I say to you, whoever says to this mountain, "Be taken up and thrown into the sea," and does not doubt in his heart, but believes that what he says will come to pass, it will be done for him.'" (Mark 11:23)

Jesus is teaching us that we must put our faith in God more than our own ability to solve a mountain of problems or circumstances in our life. Asking for God's help is something almost everyone does in difficult times. You know the old saying, "there are no atheists in foxholes." However, receiving God's help is just as important as asking. Receiving requires us to trust in God's ability and not our own. It requires us to have faith that God is a good Father and will help us.

It is one level of faith to know that God can do something in your life. It's another level altogether when you ask Him and believe that you have already received it when all you can see is a mountain of problems. "Therefore I tell you, whatever you ask in prayer, believe that you have received it, and it will be yours" (Mark 11:24).

I had been a pastor of a local church in Southern California for five years when we felt the Lord leading us to get a larger building. We were meeting in a school and had ninety people coming on Sundays, including children. We needed a bigger space to grow. Taking a step of faith, I went on a drive after church one Sunday and found a large warehouse near the Angels' stadium. As I walked around the building, there was an open door, so I went inside. It was perfect, except for a large support beam that stood right where the pulpit would have gone. I stood next to where I imagined the pulpit would be and asked the Lord, "Is this our new home?"

"Do you want this?" the Father asked in that small voice inside me.

His question rocked me because I didn't know how we could afford it. I felt like the disciples being asked to feed a multitude with a kid's lunchbox. I knew God was offering our church a breakthrough, but I didn't know how He was going to do it. I took a deep breath.

"Yes, Father. I want this for our new home. Would You do something for me? Would You have the owners of the building offer to move the beam for free?"

I called the building owners the next day to inquire about the space, but I didn't mention the support beam. Within a few hours, I received a call back.

"Ed, we looked at the warehouse and there is a beam where you might want a pulpit to go. We will move that for free."

I got up from my desk and danced around my home office.

Our whole team felt God was leading us, so we signed the lease, set a date for our first Sunday, and got to work. We had three months to finish the build-out and raise the $550,000 we needed. Each week, faithful men and women were giving their best toward the remodeling project. The construction was the fun part, but the fundraising was much harder for me. We successfully raised over $340,000 in just over two months, but with three weeks left we were still $210,000 short to finish the build-out.

In the five years after founding the church, I had not taken a vacation. I had also promised my wife that I would take some time to rest. She was urging me to take some time off now, because she saw the stress I was putting on myself and she was concerned. Worry was keeping me up at night, and I was afraid that I had foolishly stepped out to get a building we could never afford as a small church. I knew that God loved me but didn't fully understand that He loves being generous with us. Though I had read it many times, I didn't really understand this verse:

> "If you then, who are evil, know how to give good gifts to your
> children, how much more will your Father who is in heaven
> give good things to those who ask him!" (Matt. 7:11).

The reason I was struggling was because I grew up believing that there was not enough money to pay for what we wanted and sometimes even what we needed.

I remember a moment, early in my story, when I asked my stepdad for a new baseball glove. He said, "There is not enough, son. We can't afford it." I heard that response from him over and over as I grew up. I heard it so often that I learned not to ask, because "there is not enough." I wanted a baseball glove, so I got a job as a paperboy and worked until I could buy my new glove, which reinforced my newfound belief system that "if it is going to be, then it is up to me." In one way, this was a good lesson for me. It taught me that if I worked hard, I could earn the things I wanted or needed. I learned that hard work is good for the soul. What I didn't learn about hard work is found in James 1:16-17:

"Do not be deceived my dear brothers and sisters. Every good and perfect gift is from above, coming down from the Father of heavenly lights, who does not change like shifting shadows." (James 1:16-17, NIV)

I found it much easier to believe that verse for other people than I did for myself. I have watched God's good and perfect gifts bless many people through the years. He was the one who blessed me with the paper route. He was the one who blessed me with living my dream of playing in the NFL. Not every kid who wants to play in the NFL realizes that dream. I am so grateful for His blessings in my life. But God put me in a circumstance where He would teach me that He is a good Father who loves to be generous with us.

We all learn things from our childhood that shape our belief systems, some true and some not. I had a limiting belief about myself and God that was not true. I was limiting God's blessing to the area of finances because I didn't think He could bless me unless I did everything right. So my belief wasn't true. "If it's going to be, it's up to me" was a flawed thought. I needed to learn a new truth: "If it's going to be, it's up to me learning how to receive all I need from my generous Father in heaven, His good and perfect gifts from heaven."

If You Rest, I Will Work

My wife knew I needed a break. She scheduled a vacation for the family for the final two weeks before our first Sunday in our new—still unfinished—building. I didn't want to go. I hadn't been sleeping, and as I struggled with my lack of faith, I allowed anxiety to take the place of my trust in God. I felt it was my personal responsibility to make sure we got all the money we needed. I felt it was my responsibility to personally oversee the completion of the work before our first Sunday. We still needed $210,000. I was way short of my goal and did not see a way to raise the $210,000 we needed to finish. I felt like a failure. Wasn't I the pastor of the church? Hadn't I heard from the Lord? When I resisted the vacation, my wife said to me, "Ed, why don't you trust God and let Him answer this need we have? You have worked hard and have done everything you can do." I knew she was right, but I still felt as though I was responsible for making sure God followed through.

Driving to work the next day, I felt God speaking to my heart. He said, "Ed, if you rest, I will work. If you work, I will rest."

Although I was still struggling to trust God, I began packing for vacation. While I was packing, I got a phone call from one man in our church. He said he knew that I was planning to go out of town, but he needed to speak to me before I left, if possible. He noted it was very important that I come in person. I drove over to his apartment as quickly as I could as my whole family was now ready to head out for vacation.

As I sat down at his kitchen table, he said, "How much money is still needed to finish our church build-out?"

I was surprised by his question because I'd assumed he'd called me over for a counseling appointment to discuss some problem he was having. I told him how much it would cost to finish our building without the extra expense of carpet in the hallways and the sanctuary. I was still so lacking in faith that I gave him the bare minimum we needed to finish the building.

His next question was even more shocking: "Yes, but how much do we need to finish the building, including the carpet?"

When I answered him with the entire $210,000 amount, he excused himself and left the room. A few minutes later he came back with a $150,000 check and told me that he would give the rest on Sunday. I was so overcome with the faithful provision of the Lord I nearly fell out of my chair.

As I left with my family for vacation, I was reminded of the words of Jesus: "Come to me, all who labor and are heavy laden, and I will give you rest" (Matt. 11:28). Learning to trust and receive from God is a continuous process that we learn from over a lifetime. We don't wake up one day having arrived as a great dad, husband, father, or leader. It's a journey where the more you receive the goodness of God, the more you become just like Jesus. It was a humbling moment for me, because I wasn't the one who made it happen. Miracles can have that effect on us. "Come unto me" is all about receiving—not producing. The promise of Jesus is, "I will give you rest." God wants us to come and receive from Him, and in that position of receiving, we become more like Jesus.

I was struggling with learning to receive because I was still living from my old "like father, like son" story with my dad, where I was taught that if it's going to be, it's up to me. It is the same story he learned from his father. I struggled receiving from God because I still believed I had to make everything happen on my own. Sound familiar? Jesus came not only to save us through His mercy, but He also came to give us a brand-new "like Father, like son" relationship—the same relationship that Adam and Eve had with the Father before they sinned against God and lost relationship with Him.

That was a huge discovery for me when I realized that in Christ I could have the same relationship with God as my Father that Jesus had. When Jesus called me to come to Him, He was calling me to a whole new way of becoming a man, husband, and father. He was calling me to turn over the reins of my life so that I could rest in Him by giving Him the burdens of my life I am struggling to carry. Jesus said:

> "Come to me. Get away with me and you'll recover your life. I'll
> show you how to take a real rest. Walk with me and work with
> me—watch how I do it. Learn the unforced rhythms of grace."
> (Matt. 11:28–29, MSG)

When Jesus says that He will give us rest, He's calling us into a whole new "like Father, like son" relationship where we are no longer forcing our way through life but are following the unforced rhythms of His grace. They are unforced because they are received from the Father. Jesus was the first man to ever walk on the earth who was completely committed to being fathered by God like Father, like Son. He invites us to receive the same way He did.

Learning to Follow

When Moses led the children of Israel out of Egypt, there were "about six hundred thousand men on foot, besides women and children" (Exod. 12:37). The men they counted would have been of military age and ability. Some estimate the total number of people to have been around 2.4 million. Moses had years in the wilderness with God, yes, but the moment he went back to Israel, it was game on. He was not only learning to become a leader; he was also thrown into a leadership role over 2.4 million people, not all of whom were Moses backers or God followers. There were a lot of people in that crowd who were just looking to get out of Egypt. He had been called to lead a group of people who were not convinced of his ability to lead them.

After the plagues and the exodus from Egypt, the Israelites came to a dead end. They had the Red Sea on one side and the approaching Egyptian army on the other. It terrified the people. As the Egyptian army drew near, the people said to Moses,

> "Is it because there are no graves in Egypt that you have taken us away to die in the wilderness? What have you done to us in bringing us out of Egypt?" (Exod. 14:11-12)

I don't think Moses had any more idea than they did of what the Lord was about to do. Learning to lead is more about following and trusting in the Lord's provision than your ability to always have an answer. Moses had a secret history of God's faithfulness to him, which enabled him to trust that the deliverance would come from God. It doesn't appear Moses was threatened by this contempt from the people he was leading either, as he responded,

> "Fear not, stand firm, and see the salvation of the Lord, which he will work for you today. For the Egyptians whom you see

> today, you shall never see again. The Lord will fight for you,
> and you have only to be silent." (Exod. 14:13-14)

What a statement! "The Lord will fight for you, and you have only to be silent." Moses declared God's protection and promises over the people of Israel. Moses was trusting God to be the deliverer of the Israelites by receiving all the grace he needed from the Father—the true deliverer of Israel—and proclaiming it to the people. Speaking God's promises over your life and family, like Moses did, can change the future.

Shortly after the crossing of the Red Sea, the Israelites found themselves in the wilderness with no water. After three days, they finally came to Marah, where the water was bitter and they could not drink it. And they grumbled against Moses again. Even having personally viewed and experienced the plagues of Israel and their deliverance through the Red Sea, the people were still complaining.

> "And Moses cried to the LORD, and the LORD showed him a
> log, and he threw it into the water, and the water became sweet."
> (Exod. 15:25)

The word *Marah* means "bitter," and bitterness destroys the usefulness of both water and human life that is poisoned by it. The people of Israel stopped trusting in the goodness of God and only saw the bitter waters. Moses cried out in prayer to the one who made the waters. He didn't take matters into his own hands to solve these challenges; he had learned to ask God for help and do exactly what He told him to do.

There was nothing magical about the piece of wood; it was Moses' obedience to the Lord and God's power that produced the miracle. It's interesting to me that the Lord told Moses to throw a log into the water before the water became sweet. This is a picture of the cross of Jesus: like the log, He is the only way to make bitter waters of our lives taste sweet.

As many of you know, the complaining of the Israelites didn't end there. They complained about the lack of food, they complained about the miraculous food that God provided (manna), they complained about the giants in the land, and they complained about the leadership of Moses. However, Moses learned not to take complaints personally by going to the Lord to receive answers and solutions.

Too often I have taken my wife's or kids' complaints about me personally rather than taking all of those things to the Lord. Here's a secret I have learned when my family is going through a hard time—rather than participating in the blame game, I acknowledge the complaints and challenges with them before the Lord. We take it to the Lord in prayer together. This helps me not take everything that's going wrong personally (even if they all think it is my fault) and it also helps reframe the problem for my children. Where do we go when we have problems? Do we complain to our parents or management? Do we rant on social media? Or do we take it to the Lord in prayer and open ourselves up to receiving His direction?

Trusted Men

This is an important part of the Receiving Principle: we need to go to God in prayer with an open heart to receive the answer we need. We need to keep ourselves in a place of receiving so that we not only hear from the Lord but also act on what we learn from Him. When we enter into that lifelong journey of becoming the men, husbands, and fathers God has called us to be, we need to keep ourselves in a continual place of receiving from the Lord, because there is always another opportunity to improve and become more like Jesus.

At one point, while leading the Israelites, Moses' father-in-law, Jethro, came to visit Moses. Jethro had watched as the people brought their problems to Moses to judge them. Remember, there were over 2.4 million people at this time, all living in one area together. Moses was essentially doing the job of our local government and church—disputes between neighbors and questions about

God's law—all by himself. When his father-in-law saw this, he said, "What you are doing is not good. You and the people with you will certainly wear yourselves out, for the thing is too heavy for you. You are not able to do it alone" (Exod. 18:17-18). Moses was still thinking he had to become a bigger, better leader. Imagine a man who had been trained in the house of Pharaoh trying in his own strength to lead the people of Israel. God gave Moses trusted men to walk with. Moses was still learning how to lead God's way.

Moses wasn't born as the perfect leader. He didn't always get it right, even though he was chosen and called by God to lead the people of Israel to deliverance. Moses became a leader through the process of daily going to the Father to receive what he needed. There will be mistakes on your journey to becoming the man, father, and husband that God has called you to be. Even though you may be faithfully receiving from the Father, you will still experience times of discouragement, no matter how big a man you are. Moses needed the wisdom, counsel, and fellowship of other wise men provided by the blessing of the Father to help him as he led the people God had called him to lead. "Iron sharpens iron, and one man sharpens another" (Prov. 27:17).

Moses needed those trusted men and God's direction every day. I meet men who feel all alone in their stories all the time—men who want friends but, because they have invested so much of their life in performing in their careers, feel isolated. It's common for us men to put on the front of "I've got everything together; everything is under control." When people ask us how we are doing, we have a reflex answer: "Doing good! Feeling like a young lion today." Sometimes we feel like saying, "Not so good. I'm really struggling today." But we don't have trusted friends we can open up to with our weaknesses and challenges.

One thing God put in Moses' life was a small group of men who had his back. Do you have a group like that? I do! It has been one of the joys of my life to grow older with a group of men who pray for me and want to honor God in everything they do. Being in a small group of men every week is one of the most important things you can do to keep yourself connected. A good place to find a group of men to befriend is in your local church. Join the Men's Bible Study if they have one, or ask the pastor to point you to someone you can pray with.

Leading While Learning

After His death and resurrection, Jesus told His disciples, "Do not leave Jerusalem until the Father sends you the gift he promised, as I told you before. John baptized with water, but in just a few days you will be baptized with the Holy Spirit" (Acts 1:4-5, NLT).

And Jesus did just as He promised He would. The book of Acts is the story of the Holy Spirit being poured out upon the followers of Jesus. The crowd that witnessed the outpouring of the Holy Spirit, complete with tongues of fire and men praising God in different languages, thought they must all be drunk. Peter stepped forward and spoke to the crowd about Jesus Christ. Three thousand people were baptized and added to the church that day.

This moment was significant in the life of Peter. During His time on Earth, Jesus said, "And I tell you, you are Peter, and on this rock I will build my church, and the gates of hell shall not prevail against it" (Matt. 16:18).

But after Peter's denial of Jesus, I'm sure no one, least of all Peter, really believed that Peter would be the head of the church. God's thoughts are so much higher than ours, aren't they? The prophet Isaiah, speaking of God, wrote, "For as the heavens are higher than the earth, so are my ways higher than your ways and my thoughts than your thoughts" (Isaiah 55:9).

On that day of Pentecost, Peter, the least likely candidate from Peter's perspective, became the leader of the early church. Peter was able to become the leader because he was open to receiving all the grace and power he needed from the Father and His Son—the true head of the church.

Learning to receive is tied directly to our ability to listen to God's voice. Those of us who tend to trust in our own ability may have difficulty hearing God's voice. "For God speaks in one way, and in two, though man does not perceive it" (Job 33:14).

God is constantly speaking to us and we sometimes don't perceive it. Learning to listen for His voice is one of the most important things you can do as a man in leading your family. We can never become the leaders God has called us to be unless we value hearing His voice more than our own. Learning to listen to God's voice is crucial to our ability to follow Him into the life we have been made for.

One of the daily exercises I do to open my ears to God's voice is to read His Word out loud over myself. Getting into the habit of hearing God's Word spoken over ourselves conditions our ears to hear His voice.

Peter learned to follow the voice of the Father in his early days of leading the church. After the pouring out of the Holy Spirit on Jesus' followers, the church expanded throughout Jerusalem, Judea, Samaria, and to the end of the earth. As tens of thousands became followers of Jesus, a violent persecution erupted. The persecution scattered Jesus' followers "to the ends of the earth" and the whole world began to hear the gospel. As the gospel spread, more and more Gentiles were being saved. This was challenging for Peter because he had been taught that Gentiles were outside of God's favor.

God wanted to open Peter's heart to the Gentiles. Peter thought Gentiles were unclean, as did the Jewish people.

God spoke to a Gentile named Cornelius, who saw an angel in a vision say, "Cornelius." Cornelius stared at him in terror and said, "What is it, Lord?" And the angel said to him, "Your prayers and your alms have ascended as a memorial before God. And now send men to Joppa and bring one Simon who is called Peter" (Acts 10:3-5). Cornelius then invited Peter to come to his home.

God then spoke to Peter, giving him a vision he had difficulty with. In the vision, Peter saw animals of every kind, specifically animals that the law forbade the Jewish people to eat. He heard a voice tell him, "Get up, Peter, kill and eat!" But Peter said, "By no means, Lord, for I have never eaten anything unholy and unclean" (Acts 10:13–14, NASB).

Like many of us, Peter's beliefs challenged his willingness to listen to God. The voice spoke to Peter a second time and said, "What God has cleansed, no longer consider unholy" (Acts 10:15, NASB). Though it was difficult for Peter, he listened to God and learned to accept Gentile believers as God's beloved sons and daughters too.

The next day Peter brought a couple of brothers from Joppa to go to Cornelius's house, and while speaking to them,

> "No sooner were these words out of Peter's mouth than the Holy Spirit came on the listeners. The believing Jews who had come with Peter couldn't believe it, couldn't believe that the gift of the Holy Spirit was poured out on "outsider" Gentiles, but there it was—they heard them speaking in tongues, heard them praising God." (Acts 10:44–46, MSG)

Peter was learning that his success as a leader was connected to his willingness to listen to God's voice and follow Him, no matter how uncomfortable he felt doing it. When the Holy Spirit fell upon Cornelius and His entire family, Peter realized how big the Father's heart was. God's heart was bigger than just bringing salvation to the nation of Israel. God loves all of mankind.

Because Peter was willing to listen to God's voice and follow his direction, he received God's blessing as the leader of the early church.

When Jill and I were still newlyweds, we moved into a small duplex that was the perfect size for our growing family. Our neighbors were two men—a gay couple. I said things about them to my wife that made her cringe. My lack of compassion shocked her. I was uncomfortable and hardhearted. Like Peter, there was a broken place in me that was looking at people through a religious lens, forgetting that we all need God's love and mercy. I did my best to avoid our neighbors until one day one of them knocked on our door. With tears in his eyes, he asked, "I know you're a Christian. Is there anything Jesus can do for my partner? He has AIDS!" My heart broke over my sin. I had been so wrong.

I fell to my knees in front of him and said, "My heart has been wrong in the way I have judged you. Will you forgive me?"

My neighbor grabbed my hands and said, "I forgive you."

I spent the next year getting to know my neighbors and praying for them and with them. The following year, when my neighbor died of AIDS, his partner invited me to do his memorial service. God did something really powerful in my heart during that time. Like Peter, He was showing me that no one is too far away from His mercy. Jesus came to seek and save all those who are lost. Our job is to share the good news about Jesus so they can encounter Him and be born again.

Receiving While Leading

A large part of becoming the man, father, and husband God has called us to be depends upon our willingness to receive. We need daily time with Jesus so that we can receive the grace we need to be the husbands and fathers our families need.

Like Peter, we need to be humble enough to change direction when we feel God is confronting a broken area in our life, and to trust Him leading us into a new adventure. Sometimes God uses our wives and children to speak to us. Keeping our hearts open to them, even when they are pointing out a flaw in us, can be a challenge for us. We have to give up our desire to respond and correct and just listen for what God might be trying to say to us through them. Learning how to reach our families, especially after we have hurt them, requires deep humility. Reconciling with them is more important than being right. Authority without compassion will keep our families broken, but compassion with understanding becomes the bridge we need to reconcile with our children. There will be times when we are corrected by others who are listening to God—maybe even by our own wife or kids. We don't have all the answers on our own.

The book of Proverbs says, "The reward for humility and fear of the Lord is riches and honor and life" (Prov. 22:4). The Father will honor humility in your life and your willingness to look to God and other godly men for wisdom.

As husbands and fathers, it can be tempting to think that we need to have all the answers in order for us to have the authority and respect we desire. That's our old "like father, like son" syndrome talking. The goal is to receive just like Jesus did, just like Moses did, just like Peter did, so that those around us will look at us and see how God the Father and His Son are changing our lives. We need to have the humility and willingness to keep receiving from the Father to become the man, father, and husband that our family needs.

When the Father spoke those words, "Ed, if you rest, I will work. If you work, I will rest," He wanted to change something I believed that wasn't true. God used that experience to show me that I still had barriers in my mind. Even though I knew I should trust Him with raising the money we needed, in my heart I still didn't fully trust Him. I thought I had to make it happen by my own efforts rather than depending on God.

Nothing comes close to knowing and receiving from Christ Jesus. The more we get to know Him, the bigger He becomes in our lives and the less we rely on our own abilities. That's one secret to receiving: the more we receive from Him, the more we become like Him. To me, this verse is an invitation to make my life less about me and more about Jesus. What about you?

Personal Insights

1. Are you depending on yourself too much?
2. Are you showing humility, like Peter did, while leading your family?
3. Where is God calling you to be less of you and more of Him?

Key Takeaways

Consider these words of Jesus:

> "Truly, truly, I say to you, the Son can do nothing of his own accord, but only what he sees the Father doing. For whatever the Father does, that the Son does likewise. For the Father loves the Son and shows him all that he himself is doing." (John 5:19-20)

Jesus lived out His life as a Son who followed every move His Father in heaven made. He demonstrated the ultimate example of humility by coming to the earth in the form of a man and giving His life to save us. Like Father, like Son! Jesus came to follow His Father, and He is inviting us to do the same thing. God's power comes to us in those moments when we follow and do what the Father is calling us to do.

How To's

1. **How do you trust God enough to receive while leading when your hair's on fire?**

   Carefully and thoughtfully read this scripture:

   > "Rejoice in the Lord … The Lord is at hand; do not be anxious about anything, but in everything by prayer and supplication with thanksgiving let your requests be made known to God. And the peace of God, which surpasses all understanding, will guard your hearts and your minds in Christ Jesus." (Phil. 4:5–7)

   The Bible says here that "The Lord is at hand." I remember coming upon this scripture years ago, reading "don't be anxious about anything," yet my hair was on fire and my world had gone sideways. The idea I took from this scripture for years was that if I could just pray enough, then I wouldn't be anxious. What I didn't realize at the time was that the scripture actually starts in verse 4 where it says, "Rejoice in the Lord … the Lord is at hand." That is why we should be anxious about nothing. That's also why we rejoice in the Lord, because He's at hand! Because He is present, we don't have to worry about anything. He's got our back for everything that we are anxious about.

   This helped me realize that being anxious happens when I believe that I have to do everything right as a dad and husband on my own. I have to be the best leader of my life. I have to handle my company, my job, and my finances on my own. But when I turn to prayer, understanding that God is at hand, guess what happens? Look at the promise here in this verse: "the peace of God that passes all understanding will now guard your heart and your mind in Jesus Christ." There is a supernatural transaction that happens in our prayer lives when we start with "the Lord is at hand" and know that our Father in heaven has our backs. Since He is at hand, all we have to do is give Him all the things we are anxious about with thanksgiving. "With thanksgiving" means that we are thanking Him before the answer comes because He's at hand and we know that He is a good Father who has our backs.

> **To learn more about how God has our backs,**
> **I recommend reading *The Difference A Father Makes.***
> Access a free copy here blessingofthefather.com/freebook

2.   How do you live with less of you and more of Him?

Connect to God every day by praying, reading, meditating on His Word, and declaring the promises of God out loud over your life. When we make time for Him every day, He will turn our hearts from ourselves to Him. This is the most important appointment we have every day.

So how do you declare the promises of God over your life? Give yourself time every day to read the Bible out loud. While you read your Bible, the Holy Spirit will highlight something to you from God's Word. It might be something you're not doing, or something He wants you to do, or a promise He has for you. Take those things in that scripture and turn them into prayer and declare them out loud over your heart.

Here's an example: "For I know the plans I have for you, declares the LORD, plans for welfare and not for evil, to give you a future and a hope" (Jer. 29:11). Now, take that verse and turn it into a prayer like this: "Father, I know that You have plans for me. I know that You have a great hope for me and my family. I trust You and ask You to open my heart and mind to see the plans You have for me and the hope You have preserved for me, in the name of Jesus, amen."

When you pray God's inspired Word out loud over your life, it's the same as God speaking those things out of His mouth. Remember, He wrote the Bible by speaking to men so that they could write down His words. Timothy wrote:

> "All Scripture is breathed out by God and profitable for teaching, for reproof, for correction, and for training in righteousness, that the man of God may be complete, equipped for every good work." (2 Tim. 3:16–17)

Something powerful happens in our hearts when we hear God's Word spoken over our lives, because "faith comes from hearing, and hearing through the word of Christ" (Rom. 10:17).

The more you fill your heart with the Word of God, the more equipped you will be to become the man, husband, and father your family needs.

Our free daily devotional will help you fill your heart with the word of God every day.

Access it here:

https://www.blessingofthefather.com/daily-devotional

Prayer

Father, thank You for showing me that You have a great future and hope for me and that my me-centered life is not the life that You made me for. I've spent too much of my life thinking I had to make things happen instead of receiving You to become the man, husband, and father You called me to be. I open my heart and ask You to speak to me and change me and give me the grace I need to humble myself and follow You instead of trying to lead my life without You. In Jesus' name, amen.

CHAPTER 6

RECEIVING: THE BLESSING OF THE FATHER

*"...the deepest search in life, it seemed to me, the thing that in
one way or another was central to all living was man's search to
find a father...not merely the father of his flesh, not merely the
lost father of his youth, but the image of a strength and wisdom
external to his need and superior to his hunger, to which the
belief and power of his own life could be united."*

Thomas Wolf, *The Story of a Novel*

Receiving a blessing from our father is one of the most powerful things we can receive. Something happens inside of us as men when our dads believe in us and tell us we were made for a purpose. But something far greater happens when we discover that the Creator of the universe wants, as a Father, to bless our lives and give us everything we need to fulfill our calling.

A blessing is received in someone's life when they hear and receive the words of blessing that are spoken over them. God made us word-activated human beings. The words spoken over us either unlock our capacity as men or women or limit the way we see ourselves. The words of our fathers have either blessed us toward unlimited potential or left us second guessing who we are and wondering what we were made for.

What were the words your father spoke over your life? Maybe your dad knew how to bless you with his words and call you out to be a man. Or maybe he didn't. I have spent many death-bed last moments with sons and their ailing fathers where the son is still waiting for his dad to bless him. God has made all of us to receive a father's blessing. When a father doesn't know how to bless his kids, it's often because he doesn't feel like he has a blessing to give. God the Father always has a blessing to give if you are open to receiving it.

God's intent with sending His Son was not only to save us from our sins but also to add us to His family so He could be our Father. Notice how the apostle John describes this incredible blessing to those who received Jesus:

> "But as many as received Him, to them He gave the right to become children of God, even to those who believe in His name, who were born, not of blood nor of the will of the flesh nor of the will of man, but of God." (John 1:12-13, NASB)

Notice we must "receive" Jesus to become the children of God and realize the blessing of the Father. This incredible blessing of the "right to become children of God" is why Jesus promised us, "I will not leave you as orphans; I will come to you" (John 14:18).

Jesus called everyone in the room that day an orphan. He wasn't talking about people who grew up without a father in their story. He was talking about people who were born as sons of Adam, without God as a Father in their life. In Hebrew, the word for "orphan" (יָתוֹם, yā̱tom) means "fatherless." When He said, "I will not leave you as orphans," He was making a promise to His disciples that they would not be fatherless but experience the same love from God the Father as Jesus did, as God's Son:

"I made known to them your name, and I will continue to make it known, that the love with which you have loved me may be in them, and I in them." (John 17:26)

Jesus' promise was a new beginning for the disciples, and it is a new beginning for us. When we receive Jesus, we also receive our adoption as beloved sons and daughters in Christ. Included in that adoption are all the same blessings that Jesus received from the Father: "… who has blessed us in Christ with every spiritual blessing in the heavenly places" (Eph. 1:3).

Many Christians, including myself in my early years, have accepted Jesus as their personal savior but have never fully understood that His death also gave them the right to become children of God. The Father sent His Son to save us so that He could adopt us and heal the deep wounds of fatherlessness caused by Adam's sin.

The Fatherless Wound

In the early days of my oldest son's golf career, as we stood on the course one beautiful sunny day, one of his teammates walked up to me and said, "Could you be my dad? My dad has never come out to watch me compete. I've watched the way you are with your son; I just wish that I could have had a dad like you."

His words stunned me. He suffered from a fatherless wound. I wish I could report that this was an isolated story, but I meet people every day whose fathers were so preoccupied with their own stories that they never learned to be part of their kids' stories.

Our world is bursting with boys and girls who are hungry for a loving, present father. No matter how old we are, we never stop needing or wanting a father in our story. God made us to be named and blessed by our fathers, and when we miss out on that, we try to replace that father/son relationship with everything and anything we can.

There is much written today about the depth of the wound of fatherlessness. Below are some remarkable statistics regarding the damage done by fathers who were physically or emotionally absent or, even worse, abusive:

- According to the U.S. Census Bureau, 19.7 million children, more than 1 in 4, live without a father in the home.

- 47.6% of children from fatherless homes live in poverty, which is 4 times the risk of children from two-parent homes with fathers. (U.S. Department of Health and Human Services 2014)

- 63% of youth suicides are from fatherless homes, 5 times the average. (U.S. D.H.H.S., Bureau of the Census)

- 85% of youth in prison are from fatherless homes. (Fulton County, Georgia, jail populations, Texas Department of Corrections, 1992)

- 70% of teen pregnancies happen in fatherless homes. (Source: David T. Lykken, "Reconstructing Fathers," American Psychologist 55, 681,681, 2000)

- 90% of all homeless and runaway children come from fatherless homes, 32 times the average. (U.S. D.H.H.S., Bureau of the Census)

- 85% of all children who show behavior disorders come from fatherless homes, 20 times the average. (Centers for Disease Control)

- 80% of rapists with anger problems come from fatherless homes, 14 times the average. (Justice & Behavior, Vol. 14, p. 403-26)

- 71% of all high school dropouts come from fatherless homes, 9 times the average. (National Principals Association Report)

- Daughters of single parents without a father involved are 53% more likely to marry as teenagers, 711% more likely to have children as teenagers, 164% more likely to have a pre-marital birth, and 92% more likely to get divorced themselves.

The fatherless wound that began when Adam broke his relationship with the Father has plagued mankind ever since. Today the fatherless wound is deeper than most of us are aware of, and it is responsible for the leading social problems of our society. The fatherless wound desperately needs healing.

Looking at these statistics you might have been thinking, *I was one of those kids who didn't have a dad in his story.* Or maybe your dad was present physically but emotionally absent. Or even worse, maybe you were abused by your dad. How do you heal the fatherless wound in your life so you can become the man, husband, and father that God has called you to be?

God the Father sent His only Son to open the door to the only Father who can heal the wounds inside us. Jesus' finished work on the cross paid for every one of our sins and gave us the right to become children of God. If the wound you carry comes from your father, isn't it best healed by a perfect Dad, our heavenly Father? Jesus does not leave us in brokenness but offers us a way to wholeness. He came bearing the greatest gift: the Father's love we've always wanted. All we have to do is receive it.

Daddy, Do You See Me?

I recently attended my daughter's graduation at UCLA. The real story that night didn't come from the stage or from the speakers but from the stands, where the applause of moms and dads was like a wave that washed down over the thousands of graduates. It touched my heart to see parents make fools of themselves to get the attention of their kids.

My daughter called me on her cell phone and asked, "Daddy, do you see me?" When I heard that question—that question that every child asks—Jill and I responded by jumping up and down and waving like crazy fans! When my daughter saw us cheering, she started laughing, and the look on her face was something I will never forget. It's the same look that our heavenly Father wants to see on our faces once we realize He sees us and is cheering for us.

The blessing of our Father allowed Jesus to live from His Father's love rather than trying to earn His Father's love. Jesus lived a life that was only possible through the loving gaze and affirming voice of His Father. He lived the way we would have lived if Adam and Eve had walked away from that deadly fruit tree and continued to walk and talk with God. Since that fateful day in the garden, each of us is born a spiritual orphan. And ever since then, the Father, Son, and Holy Spirit have been executing a rescue plan to tear down our orphanage and lead us into the Father's house.

Are you ready to enter your Father's house?

Hearing the Voice of the Father

About two thousand years ago, the desert outside of Jerusalem was home to a strange guy. You probably would have smelled him coming before you saw him, the rank odor of his dirt-crusted body drifting across the sand. When he strode into view, his appearance would have confirmed the smell. Looking like a character from a Discovery Channel survival show, John—called the Baptizer by many people—wore ragged, itchy camel skins and a leather strap, which barely held the whole outfit together. His smile revealed his exotic diet, as uneaten grasshopper parts were probably stuck between his teeth. His scraggly beard had traces of wax from his last honeycomb-crunch sandwich.

He was there to baptize anyone who would listen. He would lower them under the water of the Jordan River and raise them up into a new way of living. His mission was to lead people to repentance but also to serve as the opening act to the greatest story ever told. John preached, saying, "I baptize you with water for repentance, but he who is coming after me is mightier than I, whose sandals I am not worthy to carry. He will baptize you with the Holy Spirit and fire" (Matt. 3:11). John had been telling everyone who would listen that he was preparing the way for the real star, the One who was coming to rescue His lost children and bring them back to His heavenly Father.

> "One day, as John was baptizing and the usual crowds gathered beside the river, Jesus showed up to be baptized. John began yelling, 'Here he is, God's Passover Lamb! He forgives the sins of the world! This is the man I've been talking about.'" (John 1:29–30, MSG)

As Jesus walked into the Jordan River to be baptized, John protested, "No! You're the One who should be baptizing me!" But Jesus insisted. So John placed his arms around Jesus and lowered him into the swirling waters of the Jordan River. Then he lifted Jesus out of the water, and as soon as the water cleared from his eyes, Jesus saw the heavens open up and the Spirit of God, like a dove, descending upon Him.

That's when Jesus—and everyone else gathered at the river that day—heard a voice from heaven, a voice filled with love, whose words would echo through the centuries as the final answer to the most profound of human problems: Who are we? What is our name? What are we named? For what have we been made? Is there anyone who loves us for who we really are? The voice of God sounded above the rushing of the river: "And behold, a voice from heaven said, 'This is my beloved Son, with whom I am well pleased'" (Matt. 3:17).

Those words spoken by God the Father over Jesus not only cemented the love of the Father on Jesus but also modeled how powerful a father's words can be when spoken over the life of his sons and daughters. Everything that was recorded as scripture in the Bible was done on purpose as a message of hope and healing. But the Bible becomes even more powerful in your life the moment you receive what God says and do what God is asking you to do.

God wrote the Bible so that we can discover how to become the husband and father our families need. I believe this is one of Jesus' most important moments with His father. His true identity, "my beloved Son," was what the Father wanted Him to never forget: "No matter what You go through, You're My Son. I love You and I'm going to back You up."

I didn't discover my true identity as a beloved son until I received the blessing of the Father like Jesus did in the Jordan river. I often tell people I became a man at forty. I had done most of the things our culture associates with manhood nearly a decade prior: married my beautiful bride, Jill; purchased a home; started a career; and became a father. None of those things marked my passage into manhood the way the blessing of the Father did. We define the blessing of the Father as the moment when the grace, forgiveness, and love of God the Father are poured out on our lives in such a way that we receive our adoption as sons of God. For some, this moment of adoption and blessing happens in tandem with salvation. But for myself, I had been walking with the Lord and pastoring a church for many years before I received this blessing and understood my adoption as a son of God.

When Does a Boy Become a Man?

When did I become a man? I really want to know.
Sometimes I wonder if I am. Can someone tell me so?
Was it when I smoked a cigarette out behind the school?
Was it when I joined the other guys and acted like a fool?

Was it when I took a drink of booze and drove around the town?
Was it when I made myself look big by putting others down?
Was it when I scored the final play that gave our team the win?
Was it when I finally got the "A" that made my parents grin?

Was it when I had a hot date and we did it all the way?
Was that when I became a man? Did it happen on that day?
Was it when I pledged allegiance to the flag and fought a war?

Was it when I came back home and wondered what the fight
was for?

Did it happen in the chapel when I walked the wedding aisle?
It seemed to for the moment, if we're judging by my smile.
Did it happen when my kids looked up one day and called me
"Pop"?

So now I am a man; at least that's what I'm told to say.
But if I am, there's just one thing that still gets in my way.
If so, I must ask it, and the question drives me wild –
but, if I've become a man, then why do I still act like a child?

(James Ryle, my best friend in heaven)

Manhood is not a moment you can attain; manhood is a moment when God
calls out His perfect design of you, those things He has meant you life to live in,
and blesses you with His grace to become that man—not an ordinary man, but
God's man endued with His presence, to accomplish those things not humanly
possible.

What held me back from recognizing that I was a beloved son of God or
that God was my Father prior to that point was that I thought manhood was
something I had to achieve. Manhood wasn't something God bestowed on you
through a father's blessing. But that is exactly how manhood is supposed to be
transferred. It is bestowed from a father to a son, and then from a son to his
children one day.

I understood those things; in fact, I taught them from the pulpit many
Sunday mornings! What I did not understand until the moment the Spirit of
God poured out His blessing upon me was that simply believing is not enough.
You can't believe that you'll be better and suddenly become better. You can't
believe you'll be a better dad and suddenly become a better dad. It's a process of

receiving from the Father all you need to become the man, husband, and father God has called you to be.

At age forty, I had an encounter with the Father where I finally understood that in order to become the husband and father my family needed, I needed to start by receiving my sonship—my new identity as a beloved son of God. I did not understand that the blessing of the father would heal the deepest part of me, the boy who lost his father. The only way for a boy to recover from being unfathered is to connect with the ultimate Father in heaven, who not only heals our wounds but also empowers us to become everything God has called us to be.

Encountering the Father

I remember the moment while sitting in my study when I read the verse about the baptism of Jesus, when God the Father spoke over His Son in the Jordan River and said, "This is my beloved Son, with whom I am well pleased."

Those words hit me between the eyes, and immediately a question came up in my heart: Why did God call Him "my beloved Son"? Why did He name Him the beloved? Why didn't He use one of the names that the Old Testament scriptures use, like the Prince of peace, the King of kings, the Lord of lords, the Savior of the world? But God the Father in that moment chose the word "beloved." The Greek word for "beloved" is *agapetos*, which means "my unconditional favor and love." I was curious why the Father used that word, so I went on the internet to search for an answer to my question and found a book online, that was being sold by a rabbi in New York City, titled *Ancient Bar Mitzvah*. I ordered the book and couldn't wait to read it.

The book arrived about a week later. I devoured it in one sitting because I believe the Lord showed me something very special in the word God used to describe who Jesus was: "my beloved Son." When I read the book, which describes the rites of bar mitzvah for a boy when he becomes a man at age 13, it confirmed my belief. The father at the end of the ceremony lifts his son onto his shoulders and says in Hebrew, "You are my beloved son, whom I love."

When I read those words, my jaw almost hit the floor because I understood in that moment that Jesus was being blessed by His Father in the river alongside John the Baptist. This was a moment of passage for Jesus. It was one of those transitions that Jesus had in His life where the Father's words empowered Him to become the man and savior of the world that God called Him to be. In that moment in the river, the Father blessed Him by giving Him the name "my beloved Son."

This was a revelation to me. I understood that every one of us has been called in Christ to discover and hear those same words over our life. It's what Paul writes about in the book of Galatians:

> "But when the fullness of time had come, God sent forth his Son, born of woman, born under the law, to redeem those who were under the law, so that we might receive adoption as sons. And because you are sons, God has sent the Spirit of his Son into our hearts, crying, "Abba! Father!" So you are no longer a slave, but a son, and if a son, then an heir through God." (Gal. 4:4–7)

This scripture opened my mind, and I understood that the blessing of the Father was initiated at the death of Jesus on the cross for every single one of us to receive the same blessing that Jesus walked under in His life. When we receive our adoption, we can let go of the broken parts of our story, the fatherless wounds, and the false names we have been given, and receive the ultimate blessing from God the father: adoption as His beloved son.

I remember the morning after I encountered the blessing of the Father for myself. Something had changed in the deepest part of my being. I had for the first time fully received that God had chosen me to be His son as Scripture says:

> "... even as he chose us in him before the foundation of the world, that we should be holy and blameless before him. In love

he predestined us for adoption to himself as sons through Jesus Christ." (Eph. 1:4–5)

God's love and grace poured into my heart as I read those words. He had always been there as a Father, but somehow I had missed it.

The next morning, I sat down with my coffee, pulled out a journal, and said, "God, You are my Father now, and I have a question that I have always wanted to ask a father about." I began writing down all the questions I would have asked my dad if he had lived. Questions about being a man, a husband, and a father. On each page, I would leave space after my questions for God, my Father, to answer. It didn't always happen right away. Sometimes weeks or months would go by and then one day as I was flipping through my journal, or reviewing my older entries, I would feel God the Father speaking to me.

I didn't realize at the time, but I was positioning myself as a son talking to my heavenly Father. I was not only asking Him questions, but I was also expecting Him to answer them. As a former athlete, I understood that I needed someone to lead me, to coach me, to guide me. I didn't get to the NFL on my own. I had great mentors and coaches out on the field training me. Those experiences led me to intuitively understand that I would not become like Jesus on my own. I would not become a great father or a great husband on my own. You might read all the books on how to be a great father, but it won't be the same as having your Father in heaven, your true Father, show you how. I was missing a father in my life, and I needed my heavenly Father to give me the information I was missing.

When I tell that story to people about asking questions, it becomes a powerful moment when they realize that God really wants to speak to us. I ask men all the time, "So, what is God saying to you?" Many times they give me a blank stare: "God speaking to me? Is that possible?" It is. As a matter of fact, it's one of the primary ways that God transforms us so that we can become the man, husband, and father our family needs. When we learn how to hear His voice by asking questions and expecting Him to answer, He will answer. He is a good, good father!

Time with My Father

One of the most powerful transformations that took place in me happened during my quiet time with the Father each morning. I would set aside time each day to read the Bible before anyone else in the house was up (five kids make a lot of noise!). After I finished reading, I would dedicate some time to praying and writing in my journal. I began discovering truths from God's Word that I already knew but were coming to me in a new light, truths like:

> "And we know that for those who love God all things work together for good, for those who are called according to his purpose." (Rom. 8:28)

> "Therefore, if anyone is in Christ, he is a new creation. The old has passed away; behold, the new has come." (2 Cor. 5:17)

As I read these verses, my mind reminded me of all the ways I had let my kids or my wife down and all the ways I could improve as a man. But at the same time, I knew God the Father was speaking these words to me personally. He wasn't shaming me or criticizing me. He was loving me into the truth of who I was and who He was. He was giving me—as a son—the inheritance He promised.

> "And because you are sons, God has sent the Spirit of his Son into our hearts, crying, 'Abba! Father!' So you are no longer a slave, but a son, and if a son, then an heir through God." (Gal. 4:6–7)

"Abba Father" is an Aramaic term used to describe an intimate personal relationship between a loving father and a loving son. In English "daddy" or "papa" imply a similar sense of close intimacy. This is an amazing promise for you and me. The Father didn't choose us to just save us from our sins. He chose to adopt us so that we could be His beloved children and receive His inheritance. Wow!

I had spent years studying the Bible searching for truth to apply to my life and looking for all the ways my kids and I had fallen short. I should have been looking for the Author, the Lord God Almighty, the Father to the fatherless, who wanted to speak to me personally. The Bible is a book you can read where the author is still alive. He is eternal! The Holy Spirit!

Listening and Speaking Like a Son

One of those mornings as I was reading the Bible, I felt a nudge, a small voice inside, from the Author, my Father in heaven. He asked, "What are you doing? Why are you reading the Bible like a Christian? Read My Word like a son would read a letter from his father and you will discover it is your inheritance!" Then He asked me, "How did Jesus read the scriptures?" *Like a Son*, I thought. That moment forever changed the way I read my Bible. My mind opened to God's Word in ways I had never experienced before.

How do you read your Bible? Like a son?

From that time on, my quiet time in the morning went from a Bible study I was doing to a conversation between a son and his Father. I'm not talking about an audible conversation but an internal one. I would take notes during those conversations and record them in my journal. One morning in particular, the Father spoke these words to me in a quiet internal voice: "I have said these things to you in figures of speech. The hour is coming when I will no longer speak to you in figures of speech but will tell you plainly about the Father" (John 16:25). I understood deep inside that God was confirming our relationship. It was as if He was saying, "You used to just read my Word as Holy Scripture, but the hour has come where my Word will come alive to you. Now you understand that these aren't just the Holy Scriptures but My Word to you—the words of a Father to His son."

The Bible says, "faith comes from hearing, and hearing through the word of Christ" (Rom. 10:17).

Our faith grows to the level that we hear the Father speaking to us. It's life changing for us men to hear from God—as a Father—the words so many of our earthly fathers weren't able to speak to us. Listening to God speak His heart and His Word to you as Father is the greatest gift you can give yourself. Start having your own time with the Father, His Son, Jesus, and the Holy Spirit every day. Jesus Himself often slipped away to have time alone with His Father: "And after he had dismissed the crowds, he went up on the mountain by himself to pray. When evening came, he was there alone" (Matt. 14:23).

Receiving from the Father every day has helped me more than anything else to become the man God has called me to be. During those times, God's spirit transformed me as His Word renewed my mind from my old, broken ways of thinking. When we learn to think the way God thinks, or as the Bible says, when "we have the mind of Christ" (1 Cor. 2:16), it opens us up to a world in which nothing is impossible. These conversations led to a daily practice I still continue today: declaring the truth of God's Word over myself.

Declare these words over yourself: "Because I have put on the mind of Christ, I am a beloved son. There are no longer any limitations on me from my old life. I am a new creation. My old life, those things I used to identify myself by, have passed away. The new man, husband, and father has come. All of my past, present, and future are marked out by You, Father. You can use even my weaknesses and work them together for my good. In Jesus' name."

What is the one thing that doesn't change instantly when we are born again and come to know Christ? Our memory!

The memories of the experiences we have had—good and bad—have shaped the way we see ourselves. Most of our barriers, the things that hold us back in life, are directly related to how we see ourselves and how we see God. Reading God's Word over yourself, out loud, will cause those words to bounce back off the wall and into your ears. Listening to God's Word, not just reading it but also hearing it, will increase your faith. That's why going to church and listening to someone preach God's Word are so important. Our faith muscle grows to the level that we listen to God's Word. "Faith comes by hearing the Word of God."

Spending time with the Father changed another place in my life as well: the way I spoke to my kids. I had been speaking to my kids more like a coach than a father, similar to the way my stepfather spoke to me. Most of the words that came out of my mouth were directive and corrective. How about you?

I'm not saying we need not coach our kids; coaching is a vital skill for every dad. But our tone shouldn't be coaching all the time. Our kids need to hear our voice as a loving, compassionate father as much as we need to hear God's voice as our Father. Our tone can build up or tear down.

Learning to Father My Kids

Years ago, I came home to find our garage door open and the entire garage filled with smoke. I was actually relieved when I realized the source of the smoke: my son Lukas had found my heat gun and had carefully burned his name into the carpet fibers on the garage floor. Sections of the carpet were melted, and the whole garage smelled of burning rubber. "Luka" had marked his spot. My typical reaction would have been yelling, "Lukas! What were you thinking?" But I was desperately trying to change my tendency to blast my kids when they misbehaved. Truthfully, I think God interrupted my usual train of thought, because suddenly, I was laughing. "Lukas!" I called. "You forgot the 's'!" We both laughed as he came out to the garage.

"So," I asked, "was it a good idea?"

"Probably not. Mom wasn't happy."

"Are you going to do that again?"

"No, Dad."

"Ok, so how are you going to fix this?"

The kindness and compassion of God interrupted the way I usually confronted my kids. My loud coaching style made my kids more afraid of disappointing me than anything else. My time with the Father was changing me. It *has* changed me. And now those changes were changing my relationship with my family.

The way we speak to our kids can either unlock their futures or imprison them. That journey of learning to speak like a son to your kids starts first in you embracing what the Father says about you and declaring that over yourself. The more you fill your heart with God's Word over you, the more it affects the way you speak to your kids. One very important point regarding your tone is that the tone you use with your kids will condition them for how they hear the Father speaking to them. Many children who have had a harsh father have trouble believing in a loving God because their biological father's voice or tone informs how they think their heavenly Father speaks and who they think He is.

Do you think that the way your dad talked to you has affected the way you talk to your kids or your wife? I know that my dad's words affected me in the way I spoke to my children and my wife. Some of my most regrettable moments as a young father came when I spoke words over my children that demeaned and hurt them. I am so grateful that, with God's help, it's never too late to learn to speak to my children and wife the same way God the Father speaks to me.

When my son Edward was just a young boy, about 10 years old, he did some things that pressed a button inside of me. I heard myself saying some of the same harsh words over him that I had received as a child. I crushed him because I was bigger than him and overpowered him with my words. Even while repeating the harsh words I had heard from my dad, I knew that I shouldn't have done it. It was almost automatic what came out of my mouth.

He pressed a button in me by telling me no, something I could not have said in any circumstance to my dad. If I had, there would have been hell to pay. As a result, I wounded him deeply, shaming him because I felt it challenged my authority.

I walked across the hallway after slamming my son's door in anger and heard him crying in his room. I went to my study, disgusted with myself and the way I talked to the son whom I love with all my heart. I sat down in my office and cried out to the Lord in prayer, asking, "Why did I do that, Lord?" It was a couple moments later, while praying and listening to my son crying in the next room, that the Father I always wanted spoke into my heart: "The reason you talked to your son that way is because of the way your dad spoke to you when he was angry. You've learned to hear My voice through the broken filter of your dad's voice. If you learn to hear My true voice as a Father, I will make you into a father who makes a difference."

In those next moments He lovingly showed me my life. I had one of those surreal, honest evaluations from my Father in heaven about my story. I saw how I had made my marriage about me, my children about me, my ministry about me. I had spent so much of my time trying to discover who I was through my marriage, my kids, and my career that I wasn't present for them and their stories. I remember my prayer: "Father, teach me how to be a father who makes a difference."

I have met many men who have been stuck in that same place because of the lack of a blessing and identity, which they never got growing up in their families. I meet men all the time who I know love their children and their wives but who, like me, are stuck trying to figure out who they are because they never had a dad who knew how to call those things out on them.

How about the harsh words or things we say in anger? Do you hear your dad talking inside of you? What about your self-talk? Does it sound like your dad? Have you heard yourself say things like, "That's just the way I am. I've always been that way." Often, self-talk is repeating a pattern we learned from our dads or other important people in our lives. Have you said or done things that hurt your children or wife that are similar to what your father did to you and that you promised yourself you wouldn't do to your kids or wife?

So how do we change those patterns? We have to change our own self-talk. We have to replace the old broken words with the words of blessing from our heavenly Father. I wanted to learn how to speak to my kids the same way God the Father spoke to His Son, Jesus, and now does to me. We change when we read and listen to God's Word daily. We increase the benefits of God's Word to us by declaring His truth out loud over ourselves. When we read and hear what His Word is calling us to do, then His Holy Spirit will empower us to do it.

Let me give you an example. You can read Paul's exhortation to the church of Ephesus, "Be kind to one another, tenderhearted, forgiving one another, as God in Christ forgave you" (Eph. 4:32), and think to yourself, *I will become a man who is kind and tenderhearted toward his kids and his wife.* But if you don't start receiving the Spirit of God to work those things out in you, then the next time an opportunity presents itself to be kind and tenderhearted, you will not see the transformation.

There are no self-made saints in heaven. You will not get there on your own. We all start out empty. The only way to change those places inside that are so broken is to spend more time with the Father by reading and listening to His Word.

Hearing the Father's Voice

I found it is easy to just read the Bible and not listen for how God wanted me to change. Have you ever read the Bible and thought, *Oh, this one will be a great scripture for my wife or my kids?* When those thoughts creep into your mind, you are not listening to God's Word for yourself. If you just read the Bible, you'll get information; but when you read the Bible and listen to what it means for you, and then listen to the way the Father speaks those words to you, then it'll change your internal voice. In addition to listening for application for yourself, you can also listen to hear the voice of the Father the same way Jesus did. And that, my friend, will revolutionize your life.

My goal in reading and listening to God's Word was to learn how to hear the Father's voice the same way Jesus heard it and then learn to speak it to my family the same way that God spoke to Jesus. I wanted to be a son like Jesus was when He said,

> "Truly, truly, I say to you, the Son can do nothing of his own accord, but only what he sees the Father doing. For whatever the Father does, that the Son does likewise. For the Father loves the Son and shows him all that he himself is doing." (John 5:19–20)

That is exactly what God wants to do for us. That became my new goal.

I don't want you to skip this part of the receiving process. Your wife, your kids, your family, and your community will need you to become a person beyond your ability to become on your own. Remember our cup analogy? You will have things poured into you by God's Spirit like never before. It's easy to miss this miraculous opportunity if you stay in the old habits of trying to fight your battles on your own. I meet men every day who feel completely isolated. They don't have anyone to help them walk through their struggles in their family, their marriage, or their career.

The key to this part of the Receiving Principle is recognizing that when you received Christ, you stepped into a bigger family—God's family. God the Father said, "I will be a father to you, and you shall be sons and daughters to me" (2 Cor. 6:18). God the Father made you for a relationship with Him, and if you are willing to receive His blessing, He will help you overcome all your obstacles.

Personal Insights

1. Was there a moment in your life when you can remember that your dad blessed you to become a man?

2. Have you ever read the Bible as a son hearing from his Father?

3. Have you stumbled and afterward felt disqualified from God's calling?

4. Do you have difficulty trusting God rather than your own abilities?

Key Takeaways

"Listen to these words for you from God the Father: 'and I will be a father to you, and you shall be sons and daughters to me, says the Lord Almighty.'" (2 Cor. 6:18)

God wants to be your Father. He wants to spend time with you every day so that He can speak to you. He will speak to you as you read and speak His Word over your life. He will transform you from the inside out and make you like His Son, Jesus.

Learning to receive from God is essential to fulfilling God's calling on your life. Like Moses and Peter, in order to realize our calling, we must receive God's love, mercy, presence, and power to be transformed into the man, husband, and father God calls us to be.

How To's

1. How do you receive your adoption as a child of God?

> "God planned from the beginning of time to one day take the role of the Father in your life. 'He predestined us for adoption as sons through Jesus Christ, according to the purpose of his will, to the praise of his glorious grace, with which he has blessed us in the Beloved.'" (Eph. 1:5–6)

For you to receive Him as your Father, you will want to exchange your old names for the new one the Father wants to give you. All of us have been given names by our dads or ourselves that have become our identity. For example, I used to call myself a football player, and that became my identity. That identity was destroyed when I was cut from the team.

Now it is time for your new name. This is your adoption day at the Father's house. He has planned for all of eternity to adopt you and move you into the eternal family that He is building. As an adopted child of God, your new name is "my beloved son in whom I approve"! This is an eternal name. You will never be cut from that team. You are an orphan no more.

You are not named by your family heritage, your ethnic background, the abuse and pain you have suffered, your addictions, your job, your sexual preference, or any other part of your life.

Are you ready?

The only real name by which you will be known forever is the name given to you by your heavenly Father at the moment you say, "Yes, I receive Your adoption of me as Your beloved son (daughter). You are my Father, and I will follow You the rest of my days."

When your name is "beloved son," and with His smile upon your life, nothing will be impossible for you!

2. How do you listen and speak like a son?

Jesus makes it clear that the Father wants to speak plainly to you as His adopted son:

> "The hour is coming when I will no longer speak to you in figures of speech but will tell you plainly about the Father. In that day you will ask in my name, and I do not say to you that I will ask the Father on your behalf; for the Father himself loves you, because you have loved me and have believed that I came from God." (John 16:25–27)

When you receive your adoption from the Father, through Jesus Christ, and believe that the Father loves you like He loves Jesus, it will open your heart to hearing His voice the same way Jesus did. On that day you will understand deep inside that God is confirming your relationship as His son. It is as if He is saying, "You used to just read my Word as Holy Scripture, but the hour has come when my Word will come alive to you. Now you understand that these aren't just the Holy Scriptures but my Word to you—the words of a Father to His son."

Practice hearing the Father's voice as Jesus did by reading our free daily devotional every day.
Sign-up https://www.blessingofthefather.com/daily-devotional

3. How does the blessing of the Father change a boy into a man?

A blessing is received in someone's life when they hear and receive the words of blessing that are spoken over them. God made us word-activated human beings. The words spoken over us either unlock our capacity as men or women or limit the way we see ourselves. The words of our fathers have either blessed us toward unlimited potential or have left us second guessing who we are and wondering what we were made for.

A father's words are powerful because they give permission and grace for that son to take his next step from boyhood to manhood. A father's words carry prophetic power for the life of his sons and daughters. That's why it is so important to use your words to bless your children in ways that unlock their potential.

When Jesus was baptized in the Jordan River, a powerful thing happened for you and me. When the Father named Jesus "My beloved Son of whom I approve," those same words that blessed Jesus in the river are the words that God wants to use to bless us.

Receiving the blessing of the Father as His beloved son empowers you to receive everything you need to become the man, husband, and father your family needs. When you receive that blessing and identity as a beloved son, you have what you need to love your wife and children the way God intended. You become the man God called you to be.

To learn more about becoming the man God has called you to be.
Download your free copy of The difference a Father Makes here.
blessingofthefather.com/freebook

Prayer

Father, I give You my old identity and the broken names I have named myself. I receive that I am Your beloved son because You have chosen me to be yours. I have made my life so much about me because I did not know who You were. I did not know that You were the Father I always wanted. I thank You that from the very first moments of my life, You have been pursuing me so You could be my Father—to heal and empower me to become the husband and father my family needs. In Jesus' name! Amen.

CHAPTER 7

RECEIVING: GOD'S CALL

*We are all priests before God, there is no such distinction as
"secular or sacred." In fact, the opposite of sacred is not secular;
the opposite of sacred is profane. In short, no follower of Christ
does secular work. We all have a sacred calling.*

Ravi Zacharias, *The Grand Weaver*

So, what is God calling you to do? Do you see your role as a husband or father as a calling from God? A calling that is sacred to Him and that you were created to fulfill with your life? I agree with Ravi in the quote above that every man has a sacred calling from God. When you see your life as more than going through the motions of work, family, and relationships, it will open your heart to this truth: God has called you to a sacred work and you will have to learn to receive everything you need from Him to fulfill this sacred calling. Have you found out, like I have, that every sacred calling of the Lord is impossible to do without Him? I just heard someone say, "Amen!"

Can I ask you another question? So, why is God calling you to do those things?

God made you on purpose and your life is important to Him. Before you were formed in your mother's womb, God chose you to be His beloved son. He created you to fulfill His purpose on Earth.

> "He chose us in him before the foundation of the world, that we should be holy and blameless before him. In love he predestined us for adoption to himself as sons through Jesus Christ, according to the purpose of his will, to the praise of his glorious grace, with which he has blessed us in the Beloved." (Eph. 1:4–6)

He called you to be a husband and introduced you to your wife. He is the one who called you to be a father and blessed you with children. He is the one who puts the desire in your heart to choose a career and excel at it. Those callings are all holy to the Lord!

Why does God want you to fulfill your calling? Because when you fulfill God's calling, you become part of God's great symphony of design for His family. Your wife needs a loving husband to fulfill her calling. Your children need your presence and blessing to fulfill their calling. You need your wife, children, and career to fulfill your calling—all to the glory of God the Father and His Son, Jesus Christ. When you live out the calling on your life, Christ will ultimately be seen in you.

> "Now when they saw the boldness of Peter and John, and perceived that they were uneducated, common men, they were astonished. And they recognized that they had been with Jesus." (Acts 4:13)

It is never too late for you to learn how to fulfill your calling. So let's look at the lives of Moses and Peter and discover together how God the Father shapes sons into the men He created them to be.

When God called Moses to lead the people of Israel out of slavery in Egypt, He called him to be somebody he had never been before. Like many of us, Moses did not realize what God's calling on his life was. When he realized it, he looked at his calling from the perspective of his own ability and was filled with doubt and fear. He had to learn to receive in order to become the man God called him to be. Moses had to learn that it was impossible to fulfill God's calling without His help.

Answering God's call starts with us saying yes and learning to receive everything we need to fulfill His purpose in our lives.

How does He father us into the place where we learn how to receive? How does He help us become everything He has called us to be? We all have places in our lives where we stumble, where we took our lives into our own hands and made mistakes. So how does God use those mistakes to shape us?

> "But now, O LORD, you are our Father; we are the clay, and you
> are our potter; we are all the work of your hand." (Isaiah 64:8)

This scripture about God being our Father and we the clay was really worked out in the life of Moses. When Moses was born, they sent a decree out from Pharaoh that all the sons born of Israel were to be slaughtered. His mother put him in a wicker basket and floated it out onto the Nile River, hoping to save his life. Pharaoh's daughter found him on the river and adopted him. Moses didn't grow up in his father's house. He grew up in the house of Pharaoh. Though he had all the luxuries of being a son of a pharaoh, he never got to receive the love and blessing from his birth father.

This likely produced insecurity in Moses regarding who he was and what he was capable of. He stuttered as a young boy, and that continued into his adult years. The confidence and security that would have been formed if he had been raised in his father's house were not there. Moses started out his story as an orphan. It's interesting to me how God continually takes boys and girls who have not been raised in a loving father's house and fathers them into the men and women He has created them to be. Do you think the wound of not being fathered by his biological dad affected him as the young stepson of Pharaoh?

Receiving for Moses

Moses had to overcome some serious doubts to become the man God had called him to be. When the Lord met Moses at the burning bush and called him to lead the nation of Israel, He said,

> "Come, I will send you to Pharaoh that you may bring my people, the children of Israel, out of Egypt." But Moses said to God, "Who am I that I should go to Pharaoh and bring the children of Israel out of Egypt?" He said, "But I will be with you, and this shall be the sign for you, that I have sent you: when you have brought the people out of Egypt, you shall serve God on this mountain." (Exod. 3:10–12)

Moses responded, "Master, please, I don't talk well. I've never been good with words, neither before nor after you spoke to me. I stutter and stammer" (Exod. 4:10, MSG). Even after God reminded Moses that He was the one who made his mouth, meaning, He could heal him, Moses still wasn't ready to receive it. Moses had to work through his own identity issues—the conflict between who he thought he was based upon his weaknesses and shortcomings and who God thought he was and had called him to be.

Moses learned to become the man that God called him to be by receiving everything he needed from the Father, versus trying to do everything on his own. Moses showed his reliance on the Lord when he said,

> "If your presence will not go with me, do not bring us up from here. For how shall it be known that I have found favor in your sight, I and your people?" (Exod. 33:15–16)

He's telling the Lord, "If You don't go with us, I can't go because they won't follow me." Moses understood that he could not become the man God called him to be if God didn't go with him. Moses realized he couldn't lead the children of Israel without God's presence. It was too big a task for Moses to do on his own. When we face the challenges we have to face as men, husbands, and fathers, we need God's presence just as much as Moses did. We might not be called to lead two million people out of captivity, but it feels big enough to ask our wives or children for forgiveness for something we've done.

When we ask God for help in prayer, He will answer our prayer just like He answered Moses: "This very thing that you have spoken I will do, for you have found favor in my sight, and I know you by name" (Exod. 33:17). God will not only answer our prayers, but He will also develop a relationship with us, just like He did with Moses. The sweet spot of being fathered by God is knowing that you have found favor with Him and that He knows your name.

Notice how God answers Moses' request "how shall it be known that I have found favor in your sight, I and your people?" He answers with, "I will make all my goodness pass before you and will proclaim before you my name Yahweh" (Exod. 33:19). God was saying, "My goodness and My name upon your life are all the endorsement you need to become the man I have called you to be. It is not about your capacity to be the man; it is about My unlimited capacity." God gives Moses two things in that moment: He reveals His goodness and proclaims His name.

When we understand that the Maker of the universe, God the Father, has put His name on us and also knows us by name, it's a powerful moment in our lives, because He's saying, "Consider My son, Ed [or Jeff or Josh or …]. He is My beloved son, on whom I have put My name and favor." It's like what happens when a father in front of his friends says, "Have you met my son, Jeff? He will accomplish great things. I am proud of him, and I love him. I have put my name upon him because he has my full endorsement." Those moments for a boy are extraordinary because he understands that his dad loves and approves of who he is. He understands that his dad will back him up no matter what. When you hear that from God the Father over your life, like Moses did, it makes all the difference in the world because you don't have to prove yourself to get a name. You receive a name because God has chosen you as His beloved son.

When God puts His name on you, He's giving you His endorsement. He's giving you access to all the family resources. Jesus said, "You can ask me for anything and I will give it to you." It's because the price for our sin and our adoption has been paid for by Jesus. Now as adopted, beloved sons of God, all we have to do is ask like a son and the Father will answer requests, because we are His beloved sons.

> "In that day you will ask in my name, and I do not say to you that I will ask the Father on your behalf; for the Father himself loves you, because you have loved me and have believed that I came from God." (John 16:25–27)

The missing piece for me growing up, after losing my father, was that I never got my main questions answered, the same questions that every young boy has: "Dad, what do you think about me? Do I have what it takes? What are the things that you love about me?"

God made a way through His Son, Jesus, to have all those questions answered by our heavenly Father. Even if we never had a dad, we no longer have to continue to look backward toward an earthly father to answer life's most powerful questions.

Moses initially struggled to receive God's blessing because he thought he needed to lead the Israelites in his own ability and strength. Like most men today, receiving God's help rather than relying on one's own ability is a foreign concept. We all were born trying to earn our identity from the "sweat of our brows," earning our way through life. Moses went from thinking, *I was raised to be the prince of Egypt. I should be able to do this!* To *I'm just a shepherd. There's no way I can do this.* Neither one of those identities, prince of Egypt or shepherd, enabled him to become what God called him to be. Just like Moses, we need to learn to receive God's blessing to be everything He has called us to be.

RECEIVING: GOD'S CALL   153

On the one side, you inflate your ego and pride, believing you have what it takes to overcome your challenges on your own. On the other side of pride is self-doubt and you learn to take less than what God wants to give you. You may become angry with yourself because you have fallen short in the past. You're angry because either you couldn't do it or you made the same mistake again and again. In either case, the focus of both of those mindsets is on you.

Like Moses, God wants to move us away from those prideful mindsets that are all about us and set our thoughts and minds on what God can do through us. Learning to receive is the secret to becoming all that God calls us to be. We all need the Father's help to live the life He is calling us to live. We need the Father to lead us. This requires humility on our part, an acknowledgment that we don't have what it takes without God to be the man, husband, and father our family needs.

Each time Moses spoke with the Father face to face, the Bible says his face shone with God's presence. The people saw a transformation in Moses' appearance because he had spent time with the Father. This is the "like Father, like son" transformation the Father wants to have with you and me. When we spend daily time with Him, talking to Him (praying) and listening to Him (reading His Word), we will be transformed. Time in the Father's presence will transform us just like it did Moses. We will walk away shining, so to speak, reflecting the glory of the Lord. The Father will transform us in such a way that we will look more and more like Jesus.

The incredible part about this transformation is that it's an ongoing process our wives, our kids, and our communities will also witness. They may not notice our faces shining or see the difference right away, but over time they will see us as the men who have spent time with the Father. This is probably the most incredible part of the Receiving Principle: the more we receive from the Father, the more we shine and will have to pour into our kids. The more we pour what the Father is giving us into our kids, the more they will receive from us. The more our kids can receive what they need from us, the more they will become like us—like Father, like son or daughter. It's all part of the Receiving Principle.

Receiving for Peter

Moses went to the mountain to receive from the Father and so did Peter. Jesus had already done several amazing miracles when He took Peter, James, and John up to a high mountain. While on the mountain, Jesus was transfigured before them and His clothing became a radiant white. Suddenly, Elijah and Moses also appeared, talking with Jesus. "And Peter said to Jesus, 'Rabbi, it is good that we are here. Let us make three tents, one for you and one for Moses and one for Elijah.'" Notice that Peter began focusing on what he could do, "Let us make three tents," instead of focusing on what Jesus brought him there to receive. Peter was still learning to receive rather than focusing on his own ability.

The more we receive as a son from the Father, the more we will become who God has called us to be. That is why Jesus took Peter up on the mountain with James and John, to have them receive a more complete understanding of who Jesus was, the beloved Son of God. They also received an understanding of what the smile and blessing of His Father was.

"And a cloud overshadowed them, and a voice came out of the cloud, 'This is my beloved Son; listen to him.' And suddenly, looking around, they no longer saw anyone with them but Jesus only." (Mark 9:7-8)

Up to this point, they had only heard from Jesus about who His Father was. Now they heard the Father's voice for themselves, just like Jesus did. This was a very important moment in history. This was the second time God the Father spoke an audible blessing over His Son in front of human witnesses. Peter witnessed the ultimate blessing of the Father that day. Though Peter stumbled again and needed to be restored, he would eventually understand and embrace his own beloved sonship with the Father.

The second Bible account of Jesus' teaching Peter to receive occurred on the Sea of Galilee during a storm, when Jesus called him to walk on the water. Peter stepped out of the boat and walked on the water, "But when he saw the wind, he was afraid, and beginning to sink he cried out, 'Lord, save me'" (Matt. 14:30).

He became afraid because he was relying on his own ability. He knew he could not walk on the water on his own power. The word he received from Jesus was "come." That word contained all the power and grace Peter needed to walk on water. He began to walk on the water but turned his eyes from Jesus and focused on the storm, became afraid, and started to sink. Instead of trusting Jesus' word, he began trusting his own ability and knew he could not walk on water. It's just like us men when facing tough challenges: we default to trusting in our own ability rather than trusting God to provide what we need.

Learning to receive is a lifelong process. Think about all the moments that God has taken you through hard times. Has the lesson you have learned taught you how to receive help from God? I am constantly learning and being taught by the Lord that receiving, just like Jesus, Peter, and Moses, is one of the secrets to becoming the man He has called me to be.

When Peter stumbled, Jesus kept pursuing him with His love. Peter made a serious mistake when he betrayed Jesus three times. The shame Peter felt for betraying the Messiah required him to receive restoration from Jesus. When Jesus told Peter that Satan would challenge his faith and separate him from Jesus, Peter said to him,

> "'Lord, I am ready to go with you both to prison and to death.'
> Jesus said, 'I tell you, Peter, the rooster will not crow this day,
> until you deny three times that you know me.'" (Luke 22:31–34)

After Peter denied Christ three times, Jesus looked at him and "Peter remembered the saying of the Lord, how he had said to him, 'Before the rooster crows today, you will deny me three times.' And he went out and wept bitterly." (Luke 22:61–62) You can imagine how devastated Peter must have been. Broken and ashamed, Peter must have thought he disqualified himself from serving the Lord again. So what did he do?

Feeling unworthy of his calling, he went back to fishing, the career he had before Jesus called him. Have you ever blown it with God and felt like He can never use you again? Have you felt that you have crossed the line, and it's over? That is where Peter was. But Jesus had another lesson on receiving for Peter:

> "Simon Peter said to them, 'I am going fishing.' They said to him, 'We will go with you.' They went out fishing on the boat, but that night they caught nothing. Just as day was breaking, Jesus stood on the shore; yet the disciples did not know that it was Jesus. Jesus said to them, 'Children, do you have any fish?' They answered him, 'No.' He said to them, 'Cast the net on the right side of the boat, and you will find some.' So they cast it, and now they could not haul it in, because of the quantity of fish. That disciple whom Jesus loved therefore said to Peter, 'It is the Lord!' When Simon Peter heard that it was the Lord, he put on his outer garment, for he was stripped for work, and threw himself into the sea." (John 21:5–7)

> "When they got out on land, they saw a charcoal fire in place, with fish laid out on it, and bread…Jesus said to them, 'Come and have breakfast.' Now none of the disciples dared ask him, 'Who are you?' They knew it was the Lord." (John 21:12)

> "When they had finished breakfast, Jesus said to Simon Peter, 'Simon, son of John, do you love me more than these?' He said to him, 'Yes, Lord; you know that I love you.' He said to him, 'Feed my lambs.' He said to him a second time, 'Simon, son of John, do you love me?' He said to him, 'Yes, Lord; you know that I love you.' He said to him, 'Tend my sheep.' He said to him the third time, 'Simon, son of John, do you love me?' Peter was grieved because he said to him the third time, 'Do you love me?' and he said to him, 'Lord, you know everything; you know that I love you.' Jesus said to him, 'Feed my sheep.'" (John 21:17)

When Jesus asked Peter if he loved him, it must have embarrassed him and burned his heart because he had just betrayed Him. Peter must have thought, *Do I*

*love You? Don't You realize that I just betraye♦ You, the Messiah, the One sent from Go♦?
Nothing is uglier an♦ more horrible than that.* Peter didn't understand that restoration begins when Jesus shows up in our life. That is when we need to receive
His love and mercy. Jesus' love says, "I will never leave you nor forsake you." His
mercy says, "I have already paid the price for all the failures you will commit."

I noticed something interesting about this story while writing this book.
Here it is: Jesus did not require that Peter ask for forgiveness for denying Him.
You would have thought Jesus would have said, "Peter, for Me to restore you,
you first have to ask for forgiveness." But He didn't.

Why not?

Because I think Jesus wanted to teach Peter what true repentance is all about.
It is not just our prayers for forgiveness. It is also the actions we do after we ask
for forgiveness. Repentance is not just about saying we are sorry. True repentance means that you turn and go in the opposite direction. Jesus was teaching
Peter how to receive the forgiveness of the cross and be restored. Jesus was calling him to do the very things Peter thought disqualified him: "Feed my sheep."

When Jesus restored Peter over the charcoal fire, Peter never thought in a
million years that Jesus would ever want him to be a leader of His church. Jesus
was teaching Peter how to receive what the Father had called him to become.
His three questions, "Do you love me?" were followed by three blessings: "Feed
my lambs," "tend my sheep," and "feed my sheep." Jesus was speaking into Peter
the prophetic truth of who Peter would become, the leader of His church: "Peter,
you can't outrun My love and calling on your life. You will become everything
that I have called you to be, so you might as well receive it!"

God restored Peter the moment he accepted Jesus' love, mercy, and calling.
By receiving his calling again, Peter transformed from a broken, ashamed fisherman into a beloved son and the future leader of the church.

Asking for forgiveness requires humility. But living out God's calling for
you requires even more humility, because it requires you to trust God rather
than yourself.

One thing I love about my encounter with Jesus and those I've seen with other people is that it's never too late for God to restore us, even if we feel that we have totally blown it. That's an amazing truth we learn from the life of Peter. It is never too late for God to restore us, even if we are broken, even if we run away.

As a father, it's easy for us to carry around those broken moments that we have had with our kids. We might think there is too much hurt with our wife or our kids to restore our relationship. I've watched many fathers and sons, husbands and wives come to the point of not speaking to each other. Peter is a great example that, no matter how many times we have stumbled, it is never too late to restore our relationship with God. The same is true with our wife and kids.

A Father and Son Restored

Recently, while celebrating my anniversary in Hawaii, I had a conversation with a father named Tom. Two weeks before Hurricane Katrina, his son John made his regular phone call to his mother. Since John moved out, he never had many words for his dad. That night, as Tom heard the phone ring, he answered and started walking toward his wife to give her the phone. That was when he heard his son say, "Hey, Dad, can we talk?"

As Tom told me this story, tears formed in his eyes as he talked about how hard his father had been on him as a boy. He confessed to me he'd made mistakes as a father, and he was responsible for some of the distance between him and his son John. Through the years, he was a faithful husband and a good breadwinner, but he still longed for something that eludes so many fathers.

"I wanted to be more than a breadwinner," he told me. "I wanted to have a great relationship with my kids, to be part of their story."

I've met countless dads who would give anything to reconnect with their sons and daughters, to hit the reset button on fathering. So often we repeat the broken patterns our dads gave us without noticing until many years have passed. But it doesn't have to be that way.

Tom got to the heart of his story. As he held the phone to his ear, he heard his son say, "Dad, I don't want to talk to Mom tonight. I want to talk with you."

Before Tom could think or say anything, there came a chilling question: "Dad, are you ready to bury me?"

Tom couldn't believe what he had heard and asked his son to repeat his question.

"Dad, if something happened to me, would you be ready to bury me? Dad, I feel like the Lord has shown me that I'm not going to live very long." Tom's fingers tightened on the phone as his son continued: "I wanted to call and tell you that I love you and that I want our relationship to be healed."

Over the next hour, Tom and John shared a transformative father-son experience. He told me that he had one of the most healing conversations with his son since he had moved out years earlier. He longed to reconcile and connect with the son he lost because of his own brokenness as a dad. Words of blessing, forgiveness, and love were expressed. And at the end of the conversation, Tom asked a final question: "John, if I'm going to get ready to bury you, can I ask you about your relationship with Jesus?"

John replied right away, "Dad, I recently gave my life back to the Lord, and you won't have to worry about me when I'm gone." Tom knew at that moment that all his deepest prayers had been answered. After lying dormant for so long, hope had suddenly bloomed. That's why he was able to say what came next.

"Son, I'm ready to bury you."

As Tom told me this story in Hawaii, we were watching a spectacular sunset that painted the entire sky in pinks and oranges. After watching the colors deepen and reflect off the surface of the ocean, Tom looked at my wife and me and continued: "Two weeks after that conversation, my son was on his way home when Hurricane Katrina struck. A large tree was uprooted." Here he paused and took a breath. "It fell on John's car and he was killed instantly."

In the silence that followed, John said something I'll never forget: "God knew that something deep inside me and my son needed to be healed before He took him home to heaven."

This, my friends, is Jesus' promise in action. He will never stop pursuing us with His love. He loves to restore us and reminds us that it is never too late to receive the Father's love and calling on our life.

So the question for us is, how are we doing at receiving God's love? Just like Peter, we need to receive the Father's love and mercy through Jesus Christ to gain an understanding of who He is calling us to be. We don't want to be blinded by our selfishness and self-reliance, because that is where we get into trouble. Remember, we are in the process of receiving and being transformed into the men God created us to be.

Personal Insights

1. Have you had a time in your life when you have received God's calling?

2. Do you have difficulty trusting God rather than your own abilities?

3. Have you ever stumbled and afterward felt disqualified from God's calling?

4. How is God restoring your relationship with Him and your children?

5. What is God asking you to receive right now so you can become the man He has called you to be?

Key Takeaways

How does God father us into the place where we learn how to receive and become everything He has called us to be? The sweet spot of being fathered by God is knowing you have found favor with Him and He knows your name. God answered Moses' request "How shall it be known that I have found favor in your sight, I and your people?" by saying, "I will make all my goodness pass before you and will proclaim before you my name Yaweh." (Exod. 33:19) God was saying, "My goodness and My name upon your life are all the endorsement you need to become the man I have called you to be."

How To's

1.   How can you receive your calling like Moses did?

Have faith that God loves you as a son. Ask Him in prayer to help you. Be humble enough to receive His help. Take action on what He advises you to do.

To receive our calling like Moses did, we have to become aware that we can't rely on ourselves to solve every problem. Men love fixing things and solving problems. We need to ask the Father in prayer like a son and believe that God loves us and wants to help us like any good father would.

> "Or which one of you, if his son asks him for bread, will give him a stone? Or if he asks for a fish, will give him a serpent? If you then, who are evil, know how to give good gifts to your children, how much more will your Father who is in heaven give good things to those who ask him!" (Matt. 7:9–11)

Then we have to be humble enough to receive His answers and do what He is asking us to do. Moses didn't want to lead the nation of Israel. But he was humble enough to do what God asked him to do. We must be humble too. For example, you may ask God to heal your marriage, and the Lord tells you to ask for forgiveness from your wife. Have you noticed that God's answer to most of our prayers has to do with Him calling us to change and become part of the answer?

Moses was willing to do what God asked but understood that he could not become the man God called him to be if God didn't go with him. Moses realized he couldn't lead the children of Israel without God's presence and power. It was too big a task for Moses to do on his own. When we face challenges as men, husbands, and fathers, we need God's presence and power just as much as Moses did.

2.   How can you receive your calling like Peter did?

Peter had to learn to receive from God and stumbled many times before he learned. Most of us are like Peter and have difficulty learning to receive from God. Like Peter, we often default to relying on our own ability, which causes us to stumble. But Jesus is always there to restore us, just like He did with Peter. When Peter accepted his calling from Jesus to feed His sheep, he probably didn't feel capable or worthy. Yet he moved forward and did what Jesus asked anyway.

The next time we see Peter in the Bible is 40 days later when he took a stand for Christ and began preaching to Jesus' sheep: "But Peter, standing with the eleven, lifted up his voice and addressed them: 'Men of Judea and all who dwell in Jerusalem, let this be known to you, and give ear to my words.'" (Acts 2:14)

On that day, Peter gave his first sermon where 5,000 people got saved. Not too bad for a beginner! I believe that the grace that Peter needed to preach that message came at the moment he stood up and lifted his voice. God empowers us in the same way when we stand up and do what He asks us to do. Peter took a step of faith and God backed him up. He will back you up too when you are humble enough to do what He has called you to do, even if you don't feel like it.

Receiving God's calling like Peter requires humility and faith because you have to lean into the Lord for everything, rather than your own ability.

Send me an email about what God is calling you to do
so that we can pray for you.
edtandy@blessingofthefather.com

Prayer

Father, thank You for never giving up on me and for revealing Your calling to me again. Like Moses and Peter, Lord, give me the courage to stand up and do those things that You have made me for. Help me live out my calling so that You and Your Son receive the glory due You. If I stumble, restore me and teach me to rely on You instead of myself. In the name of Jesus, amen.

CHAPTER 8

BECOMING A FATHER

So Jesus said to them, "Truly, truly, I say to you, the Son can do nothing of his own accord, but only what he sees the Father doing. For whatever the Father does, that the Son does likewise. For the Father loves the Son and shows him all that he himself is doing."

John 5:19-20

When I first read this verse, I remember my heart's cry was, "I want to know the Father the way Jesus did so I can be that same kind of father to my children." As fathers, we can only give away what we have received. I needed to be fathered by God because my way of parenting my children was more like an intense football coach than a loving father. I started learning how to father by studying the relationship that Jesus had with His Father and the tender partnership they had. I wanted to have that same relationship with my kids too. When I saw how Jesus asked questions of His disciples instead of just giving them answers, I wondered if that's the way the Father spoke to Him, by asking questions. Jesus said that He only did what the Father was doing, so His Father must have been asking questions too.

One thing that jumped out to me was that Jesus asked questions of people rather than commanding them. I remember asking myself, *Why questions?* Could it be that when Jesus was a young boy, the Father asked Him questions, drawing Him to scripture, so that He could fully discover who He was? I believe so. So, as fathers we can ask questions of our children to help them discover who God has made them to be.

Why questions? Because people learned when Jesus asked questions. We can rule our children through fear or overpower them because we have authority, but the moment we do that, we take away their voice, their ability to decide for themselves. But when we ask questions, we're helping them discover the answers for themselves. And when our children learn how to hear for themselves, that will make all the difference in the world.

Learning to Father

I grew up in a home where my dad was only present about half of the time. When he was home, he led his family like he led men under his command on the submarine. We had a lot of fun moments, but sometimes we had to "fall in line," a term my dad must have learned in the Navy. That meant we had done something we would be punished for. I thought my dad learned his authoritative style as a captain in the Navy until I met his father.

I remember a visit to his dad's house, when I was young, when I said something that got me in trouble. To correct me, they washed my mouth out with soap. I was blowing bubbles the rest of the day. Talking back was not something we had permission to do either. We didn't have much of a vote, nor did I have a lot of say on the baseball and football fields where I spent the rest of my time. One of the regular things that I heard from my dad, and several of my football coaches, was, "Son, you are not supposed to think, just perform." I was not one of those kids who enjoyed falling in line. I wanted to know why I was supposed to do this or that. I know my dad gave me the best he had, because we can only give those things we have received.

It's not surprising that I adopted this coaching style at home with my own kids, barking out orders, expecting my kids to respond—immediately. It probably won't surprise you to hear that didn't go over so well with my wife and my kids. I needed God to reprogram my brain and father my heart to help me break out of my broken style of parenting. Every dad will blow it as a father sometimes and do things that will hurt his kids. That is why every one of us needs God the Father to teach us how to become the good father our kids need.

By the time my son Edward went away to college, I had gained a little experience in fathering my kids the same way God was fathering me. God wasn't an authoritative dictator who didn't value or care about my opinion. He wasn't a military commander or a coach barking out orders, although that's how God often sounded to me. I wanted to learn to hear the voice of the Father like Jesus so that I could learn to speak to my kids the same way. It took me a long time before I began to hear His voice as a loving Father. But as I continued talking to and listening to the Father during my times in His Word, I realized how I previously heard Him was not who He was at all. I was imposing my father wounds, my broken father-filter understanding, on God.

I have learned over the years that the Father invites us to come closer to Him, to enter His tender presence, to spend time with Him. He does not demand we clean up our act first or put on a better face or prove we are winners in order to spend time with Him. I have also learned that invitations from God often come in the form of questions, longings in my heart that lead me to understand what God wants me to do.

It wasn't until I could hear God the Father's voice for myself, through Christ, that my heart started changing from being a coach, belting out instructions and to-do lists, to being a loving, present father. I believe that every father wants to be that kind of dad. We love our children, and we want to make the most significant difference possible in their lives so that they can become everything that God has created them to be.

Learning to Ask Questions

This brief story is an example of how God taught me to be a loving, present father who asked questions instead of giving instructions.

My boys grew up playing and excelling at just about every sport, so it was no surprise when my oldest son received an athletic scholarship to play golf at the University of Colorado. I had spent years caddying for him on and off the golf course and was very proud of him. One morning, during his first winter away at college, I received this phone call:

"Dad, I just wanted to let you know I'm heading out with some friends to go snowboarding this weekend. I'll talk to you on Monday." The tone of his voice and his forced confidence told me he thought I would disapprove. He was correct. I wasn't happy with his plans.

Edward is our oldest son and was the first to go away to college. I could feel myself sinking into my old "like father, like son" dad mode, thinking, *You can't do that, son. Make other plans. You could get hurt, lose your scholarship, and ruin your future!* It's easy for us to project what we think is best as the only right answer for our kids. Thankfully, I had been in a long season of receiving from the Father and was learning more about being a good dad every day. When our kids are younger, they need us to protect them and lead them. When they grow into manhood, they need us to be more like consultants, helping them develop their own set of tools. I took a deep breath.

"Can I ask you a couple of questions?"

"Sure," he said.

"Did you pray about it?"

"Of course, Dad."

"Did you read your contract?"

"What contract?"

The question seemed to come as a surprise to him. As a former recipient of an athletic scholarship myself, I knew he had signed a contract with the college agreeing to certain expectations of the school.

"Your scholarship agreement." I said. "Just make sure there isn't a clause in there stating you could lose your scholarship if you get hurt in an intramural sport like skiing."

"Do you think I should do that?" he asked.

"You're a man, son. You make the call." I finally asked, "Did you ask your coach for permission? He is responsible for you and might have a problem with you skiing during the season."

"I've got to go, Dad. Thanks."

A short while later, the phone rang again.

"This totally sucks, Dad. There is a clause in my scholarship that I might give up my scholarship if I get hurt doing another sport."

He told me about his phone call with his coach, who confirmed that Edward might lose his spot on the travel team if he got hurt and preferred that Edward not go skiing. Suddenly, Edward's voice changed.

"You know, Dad, it would be totally foolish of me to risk my future as a golfer over one weekend of fun. I'm not going to go. Gotta go. Love you, Dad. Bye!"

I remembered raising my hands up and giving myself a touchdown because Jesus was teaching me a secret in how to father my son by helping him hear God for himself. It is way more powerful for our children to discover they can hear God for themselves than it is for us to tell them what they should do!

Asking questions can make all the difference with your children.

Jesus Used Questions to Teach

Jesus was always asking His disciples questions. Jesus didn't rule over His disciples like a typical leader of the day. He discipled them like a loving father so that they could learn like a son. He didn't try to overpower them with His authority to protect them from mistakes. He asked questions to help them learn how to hear from God the Father themselves. There were many places where Jesus challenged their belief systems, but He wanted His disciples to learn how to hear and do those things the Father was doing.

Questions are a powerful way for you to discern what the Father is doing in the lives of those you love. When we direct our kids and demand obedience, we take away their ability to hear from God and choose. That is why religious systems that emphasize a legalistic form of worship push people away from

God. Looking at my life as a dad, I found that, unlike Jesus, I was giving a lot of answers to questions that weren't even being asked. I was giving advice to my kids and my wife—advice they weren't asking for. I wasn't inviting my kids to spend time with me. I was driving them away by constantly demanding better behavior or other performance-oriented requests. How about you?

We have a tendency as men to want to fix everyone's problem. Ask your kids or your wife if you don't believe me! The trouble is, if we're always the one with the answers, our kids never gain the confidence to hear from God and make great decisions for themselves. Asking questions helps your kids discover the truth about themselves. Isn't that what we want for our kids? To learn how to hear God and discover His truth for themselves? Discovered truth is much more powerful for your kids than even your best instruction. Great questions will help them think through their decisions and, ultimately, train them to look to the Father for answers.

This was a crucial point in my process of receiving and becoming the man, husband, and father God was calling me to be: identifying and copying the "like Father, like Son" relationship between God the Father and Jesus. And what I noticed as Jesus represented the Father to His followers was that Jesus asked a lot of questions. And perhaps more surprising, He didn't give a lot of answers. This was a mind-blowing discovery for me. I thought back on all of my positive relationships with men I considered to be mentors or role models. What did I enjoy about my time with them? What made my relationship with them positive or helpful to me as a young man? My conclusion was this: The men who had the most impact in my life as a mentor/father were not the ones who told me what to do or what they had done; the ones who had the most impact were the ones who asked me questions about myself, my dreams, and my life—and who helped me discover who God made me to be.

That's when I started asking my kids questions. And I'm telling you, something changed in my family when I started asking questions and stopped giving answers to the questions no one was asking. It changed my relationship with my wife. It changed my relationship with my kids.

I didn't suddenly become the father who asks great questions. I asked a question or two, had some success, and then fell back into my old ways of telling my family what I thought and why I was right. There were several setbacks. My kids would tell me during those moments, "Nice sermon, Dad," which helped me know that I was pushing and not fathering them. That's how it works, isn't it? But then I asked a few more questions and over time I began to make it a practice. I would try to ask my wife and my kids questions rather than give them answers. What I realized during this time of transition was this: if you don't have the heart of your wife and your kids, they will not listen to your answers or advice, no matter how good it is. Ouch! But the good news was that my new practice of asking questions softened their hearts toward me.

Some of us have lost the heart of our wife and our kids. We've invested ourselves so much at work that we don't really know our kids. Or we've escaped into our hobbies and haven't kept the honeymoon going with our wife. Maybe you were the guy who really tried to invest in his family, but after experiencing a few setbacks or rejections, you just gave up. We've all been there. Maybe you're not even sure how you got there, but you've noticed your wife or your kids seem distant. Your kids got a little older and now you're not sure how to connect with them. Maybe your son isn't the athlete you wanted him to be. He loves video games. You aren't sure how to engage with him. Maybe you always wanted boys and you ended up with girls. You do not understand what to do with them.

You get the idea.

Some of you know exactly how you blew it. You can remember the moment it all fell apart, and you feel responsible. What do you do? Here is a story sent to me from a seat mate on an airplane flight:

> "For some time now, my relationship with my wife has been on the rocks. About four months ago, we split within our own home and I moved to the basement. I'm a national sales manager for a prominent healthcare company, and while having all the

success in the world at work, I've been an absolute failure at home.

My wife came from an abusive background, and instead of loving her through it, I became angry and bitter and traveled more and more to get away from her. I couldn't stand the sight of her or the sound of her voice, which caused me to buy the house next door to move into.

I was not supposed to be on your flight and I am so grateful I sat next to you. After a short discussion, you handed me your book *The Difference a Father Makes*. I marked it all up! Hope you don't mind!

When I arrived home, I told my family about my experience with you. I told my wife in front of the children, "I want to move back into our bedroom." She was surprised but accepted. I then told the children that I will not be leaving their mother and that I want to be a better dad. My oldest daughter said, "You're a great dad!" I responded with, "I want to become the dad you deserve, not the one you have. I will listen better, work less, and focus on you two girls."

As I tucked them into bed, my oldest daughter asked me to stay and talk. She talked and talked and talked, and I didn't say a word. I can't remember the last time that happened. The healing has begun."

How is your relationship with your kids? When my kids were younger, I hurt my oldest daughter, Jessica, because all I knew how to do was be the dad who went to sporting events. I did not understand how to be the father of girls. Recitals and performances scared me! I was much more comfortable on the field with my boys. But this devastated my daughter. I lost her heart. It was years before she taught me how to win her heart back and before I realized how much I had hurt her. She taught me so much about how to win and keep the hearts of my family. I also learned that I can have a much bigger impact on my kids when I understand what they are thinking. So I learned that asking questions is one secret to opening up the hearts of my kids again.

After years of being the dad who didn't know how to connect to his daughters, I came into Jessica's room one afternoon and asked, "Have I hurt you? Is there anything I've done that I need to ask your forgiveness for?"

She stared at me for a few moments in shock. "Really?" she finally asked.

I could see my genuine sincerity in asking was pulling up something deep within her, so I quickly added, "Well, maybe just tell me one or two things for now. I am still a man!"

She laughed as tears welled up in her eyes. It took her a few more minutes to compose herself, but as she did, she told me about how I had hurt her by not really seeing her. Although I loved my daughter, my ease with my boys and obvious support of their sporting activities came across as favoritism to her. I had wounded her deeply. I don't want you to think I asked one question during one conversation with my daughter and suddenly everything was healed and forgiven. It wasn't. It took time and many more conversations and apologies from me before we could move past it. It took a lot of listening on my part—not defending my actions or explaining my position. Sometimes the things that had hurt her were defensible or even understandable on my part. Some things she had misunderstood. But I didn't defend or explain myself. I just listened, apologized, and asked for forgiveness. The goal for listening is understanding the hurt so that you can ask for forgiveness with understanding.

"I'm so sorry for... I know that hurt you, sweetheart. Will you forgive me?"

Why Questions?

Why are questions so important in the relationships with your wife and your kids? Questions will help you reach your wife's and children's hearts, because questions reveal what's in their hearts and what God is doing in their hearts. Understanding what is in your loved ones' hearts is far more important than any guidance you might give. I discovered a hidden relationship manual in the hearts of my wife and kids when I began asking questions. All you need to do to open their hearts is ask questions and listen.

Questions helped Jesus see what the Father was doing in Peter's heart. Remember when Jesus asked His disciples what people were saying about Him or who they thought He was? "They said, 'Some say John the Baptist, others say Elijah, and others Jeremiah or one of the prophets.' He said to them, 'But who do you say that I am?' Simon Peter replied, 'You are the Christ, the Son of the living God.'" (Matt. 16:14-16) Jesus told Peter that he knew the right answer because His Father in heaven had revealed it to him. When Jesus saw what the Father was doing in Peter's heart, Jesus blessed him:

> "And Jesus answered him, 'Blessed are you, Simon Bar-Jonah! For flesh and blood has not revealed this to you, but my Father who is in heaven. And I tell you, you are Peter, and on this rock I will build my church, and the gates of hell shall not prevail against it.'" (Matt. 16:17–18)

Peter's answer to the question showed Jesus and Peter that the Father was choosing Peter to become a future leader in His church.

Jesus' questions drew out the hearts of those He was speaking to. Had Jesus answered the question for His disciples and simply told them, "I am the Son of God," Peter would not have exercised his faith and made such a bold statement. He would not have learned to hear from the Father himself, because faith isn't something we give to our kids or our family; it's something God gives them. Questions help our loved ones experience the lessons of faith they need to experience from the Father on their own. We can't do it for them.

Questions are powerful because they help to show us what God is doing in our wife's and our children's hearts. God has called every one of us for a blessing. Therefore, when we learn what God is doing in our loved ones' hearts and audibly bless what God is doing, just like Jesus did for Peter, we will see them grow to be the men and women God has called them to be. Our words carry the authority to bless or curse our families. We want to use the power of our words to bless our loved ones, because positive words of blessing help release God's calling in their lives. Using the power of our words to bless our children will do far more to shape their lives than our instruction or criticism will ever do:

> "To sum up, let all be harmonious, sympathetic, brotherly, kind-hearted, and humble in spirit; not returning evil for evil, or insult for insult, but giving a blessing instead; for you were called for the very purpose that you might inherit a blessing." (1 Pet. 3:8–9, NASB)

Words of blessing can unlock the future for our kids, but questions help us learn what is going on in our loved ones' hearts. The more we understand those things, the better we can pray for them, and the more opportunities we will have to use the power of our words to bless them. Imagine going to a doctor who gives you the cure before he knows what needs healing—not the right doctor to go to! I started out being that kind of dad; I was offering the cure because I thought I knew how to fix them before they could tell me what they wanted.

Please hear me out on this. I'm not saying you should never give your kids advice or share your opinion on things. The idea is to ask questions, following the model of Jesus to allow your kids the opportunity to work through their own faith or feelings on the subject. When you give your kids the opportunity to come to their own conclusions, when you lead them with questions, they will feel much stronger about their final conclusion. For example: "I don't believe in God because Mom and Dad said I should. I believe in God because I've come to that conclusion myself."

I am also not saying that you should never discipline your children. But the way you discipline them can make all the difference in the world. It is easy for us as dads to get angry when our children are misbehaving. When we lash out in anger, we move from discipline to punishment.

"Fathers, do not provoke your children to anger, but bring them
up in the discipline and instruction of the Lord." (Eph. 6:4)

God's goal is that we would learn how to discipline our children the way
He disciplines us. And here's the secret: He disciplines us to teach us how to
connect to Him to receive the grace and power we need to live the life He has
called us to live.

I remember getting in some serious trouble as a teenager. I had caused a fire
in the nearby forest and the fire department had to be called to put it out. My
mother sent me to my room, saying, "Wait until your father gets home! You are
going to get it!" I knew that wasn't going to be a great moment.

My father came home and was really upset with me. My dad was also embarrassed by me, which made him even angrier. My dad instructed me to "go out to
the front yard and cut off a small branch from the willow tree so that I can beat
you with it." Anticipating the punishment, I sawed off an entire big heavy branch
that I knew was too big for him to lift and hauled it through the front door. He
laughed at me and said, "Smart-ass." He was so amused by my creative way to
keep from being punished that he didn't whip me but just sent me to my room.

An hour passed before he walked upstairs to my room. I was sure I was
going to get the belt treatment. He looked at me and said, "Why did you set the
forest on fire?"

I said, "I was playing army men with my friends and we made napalm egg
bombs, like you taught us about last week. We threw too many and couldn't
stop the fire."

He looked at me and said, "When I was your age, I did some pretty dumb
things too. Are you going to do that again?"

I said, "No, Dad. I'm really sorry." He smiled and left.

When I first started disciplining my children, I did it my dad's way—which
was more about punishment than learning. I remember going to the garage with
Edward and making a paddle to use to spank him with when he was bad. I didn't
know any other way.

So I went to the wood shop with Edward and made a paddle the same way my dad had made for me. I even drilled holes in it, which causes it to whistle when you swing it. I remember my 8-year-old boy looking at me and asking, "What are you going to do with this?"

I said, "Well, if you're a bad son and do something wrong, I'm going to spank you with it. The Bible says that if you spare the rod you spoil the child." I couldn't believe that I quoted scripture.

Edward looked up at me and said, "If you hit me with this, you know I can have you arrested."

I heard myself say the same words my stepfather said to me: "Smart-ass." Fortunately, that paddle was barely ever used.

Although discipline is a good thing for our sons and daughters, punishment is not something that God wants us to use to teach our kids.

Here is a question I've learned to ask myself in the heat of the moment when I want to bring the wrath of God upon my children: Is this about punishing them so that they learn a lesson, or is this about me helping them understand what they're doing so that they choose not to do that again?

Another helpful question is, what is the Father doing with my children right now? The quickest way to understand what God is doing is to ask questions of your children. For example: "Do you know why you just did that, son? What do you think God is telling you right now?" Asking your child questions in a moment of discipline will have a more powerful effect than punishment, and it won't wound your child, causing bitterness.

That's what discipline of the Father looks like. It starts with the Holy Spirit convicting us and then God the Father offering us the grace to understand and change the broken pattern in our life.

"So don't feel sorry for yourselves. Or have you forgotten how good parents treat children, and that God regards you as his children? My dear child, don't shrug off God's discipline, but don't be crushed by it either. It's the child he loves that he disciplines; the child he embraces, he also corrects." (Heb. 12:5–6, MSG)

My goal as a dad changed from wanting my kids to do everything I thought they should do to leading my family to Christ and helping them become the men and women God has called them to be. I am discovering my calling as a father!

The Importance of Listening

We also need to learn to listen carefully to our wives' and children's questions. Their questions also reveal what is going on in their hearts. Sometimes our wives and children develop misunderstandings because of our careless words or behaviors. Paying careful attention to their questions will help you to learn how your words and behaviors are affecting them and how to heal any wounds you may have caused.

I received a phone call from a dad who was reading one of my books. As we talked on the phone, I noticed he was weeping. He said to me, "Ed, my dad left me when I was a little boy and it affected me as a man, resulting in divorce. I also know it hurt me as a father. I haven't been able to stop crying this morning because it's been almost 20 years since I have spoken with my daughter. What can I do?"

I asked him if he had tried to contact his daughter with letters. He told me that his ex-wife had blocked all correspondence and had returned his letters with a message on the outside of the envelopes: "We are dead to you!" He said, "So I just stopped trying to write, knowing that my mail was not reaching my daughter. I got discouraged and stopped writing. It has been over 10 years since my last attempt. My daughter is now in her thirties and I want to be a father who can make a difference in her life."

I prayed with him over the phone about his daughter and also about receiving the blessing of the Father. It was a very tender moment as a 55-year-old man received the blessing from God the Father that he never got from his dad. I encouraged him to write one more letter to his daughter with a request at the very beginning of the letter: "Help me understand how I hurt you when your mom and I got divorced." Next, we prayed that God would make sure she got the letter and would open her heart.

He sent the letter to his daughter and within a week he got a phone call from a daughter he had not talked to for over 20 years. She asked, "Is this you, Dad?" He said yes. After a few minutes of small talk, she said, "I have a question to ask of you but I've been waiting to ask you for 20 years and would like you to meet me so that I can ask you face to face." Her dad said yes and planned to travel to her hometown, which was hours away. They agreed to meet at a restaurant in town, and he arrived early and found a booth in the back facing the front door. He wondered what she looked like because he had not seen her for so long. He had no current pictures, only memories of his last moments with his 13-year-old daughter.

A young woman walked into the restaurant; her eyes were already filled with tears. She was looking around the room and he recognized that this was his daughter. He had waited many years for this moment. Their eyes met, and she walked over to the table and sat down and said, "Dad, I have a question to ask you."

He replied, "Okay, what is it?"

"Dad, was I that ugly?"

Her question shocked him. "What?" He repeated, "'Was I that ugly?'"

"Dad, you never held me as a little girl or showed affection to me. I don't remember you telling me you loved me. So when you and Mom got divorced, I just figured that it was because you didn't want me because I was ugly."

Her words crushed his heart, realizing that his lack of affection made his daughter feel ugly. He said, "No, sweetheart, it wasn't because you were ugly that your mom and I lost our marriage. It was because your daddy was broken and addicted to pornography. That is why we got divorced. I was unfaithful to your mother and hurt her very deeply. I was also afraid that my addiction would affect you, so I stayed away. I am so sorry that I didn't love you and show you affection. Will you please forgive me?"

His daughter almost jumped across the table, bursting into tears, saying, "Daddy, Daddy, I have missed you so much in my life. I thought you didn't want me. I forgive you!"

After about an hour of conversation, she invited him to her home, saying, "Dad, I have a gift I have been wanting to give you. Will you come by my house so I can give it to you?"

He said, "I will, sweetheart!"

After a short drive, he turned into her driveway, got out of the car, and walked up to knock on the front door. As he knocked on the door, he heard, "He's here. He's here." He watched two grandchildren he had never known he had run from the back of the house, shouting, "Grandpa! Grandpa!" They jumped into his arms as God was restoring a father to his daughter and now a granddad to his grandsons! It is never too late for God to transform our family story.

God wanted a daughter to be restored to her father, so He saved a boy named Ed Tandy McGlasson, who had lost his birth father at sea. God blessed that boy with the blessing of the Father and sowed a book into his heart called *The Difference a Father Makes*, which he published. A man from Texas who never thought he could ever see his daughter again read the book, prayed with the author, and was blessed with the blessing of God the Father. He wrote one more letter that his daughter read. His daughter called him to set up a meeting to get her question answered, "Was I that ugly?" and was restored to her father; and then her restored father was introduced to the two grandsons he never knew he had, and now that father is building a legacy with his newly restored family. Wow! That, my friends, is how God heals a daughter He loves. He uses men just like us—just like you, Dad!

A Promise to Every Father

I want to speak to those dads who have just read this story and think they can never reconnect with their children again because of all that has happened.

Let me encourage you with two things.

First, no matter how bad you think you have blown it as a dad, it is never too late for you to be a part of your children's lives. I have watched thousands of fathers learn how to become part of their children's lives again.

Even though your kids are being raised by great stepdads out there, your children will never have another birth father like you! You still carry God's authority in your life even if you have not been a good dad so far. So, don't quit; get in there. They need you in their life.

Second, your kids still need your blessing in their life. Your kids might even have said, "You are dead to me" or "I don't want or need you in my life." What they don't understand is that you as their father carry an authority given to you by God to be their father. That is why your words may have been so hurtful to your kids, because your words carry power to either unlock their destiny or imprison them like many of you have been. Whether your kids are open to you right now or not, they still have deep questions about who they are, and you can help them heal from the past—just like the daughter who thought the reason for her father's departure was her ugliness. So, how did he heal a daughter?

A Father's Calling

Dads, we are called for this. Remember what Peter said: "you were called for the very purpose that you might inherit a blessing." When we receive our inheritance of the blessing of the Father for ourselves, we now have that blessing to give to our wives and children as their new inheritance too. When we give that blessing to our children, we will experience the same joy that God the Father experienced by giving His blessing to us! I figured out that my job of being a dad is all about preparing my children to receive their own adoption as God's beloved sons and daughters. When that happens for them, they get the ultimate Father in their own story to lead them and shape them to become everything God has called them to be.

I can tell you that if you ask Him, your Father who is in heaven will inject your heart with His love for your wife and kids. He will teach you how to love them the way the Father loves you, how to pursue them the way He has pursued you, and how to lay down your life for your wife and family. You are called to bless your family the Father's way.

The key to your calling is to be open to receiving everything you need from the Father through Jesus in order to become the man, husband, and father your family needs. One of the things I've noticed about my kids as I've been on this journey is that my family has joined me on the journey. It happened supernaturally and began when I humbled myself and asked my wife and kids for forgiveness. As I began receiving and becoming the man God called me to be, my wife and my kids forgave me for my mistakes and were more open to receiving from me.

Why? Because I began to win back their hearts when I became a present dad in their story, which demonstrated that I loved them and that they were important to me. I started making life more about them and less about myself. I started taking an interest in them and what they were interested in. I began asking them questions about what they were doing, what they were thinking, and how they were feeling, and really listening to their answers. Rather than just asking my kids how their day was, I engaged with them. I stopped what I was doing, for example, and took time to watch and talk with my daughters as they were practicing for their dance recital. I played video games with my sons (even though I'm not a fan of video games). I began paying more attention to my wife and taking more interest in the things she was talking about. I had developed the bad habit of thinking about my challenges in the church when talking with Jill, rather than listening to what she was saying. So, I became more present mentally and emotionally when I was with her.

Slowly, and I do mean slowly, I won back the hearts of my wife and my kids.

There were a lot of mistakes, tears, and "Will you forgive me?" In this process, my family transformed from bitterness to joy.

Forgiveness Heals Bitterness

The Bible says, "Watch out that no bitterness takes root among you, for as it springs up it causes deep trouble, hurting many in their spiritual lives." (Heb. 12:15, TLB)

Several years ago, I went to an International Christian Booksellers convention in Denver, Colorado. We were releasing my first book. I was signing books for potential book distributors when my publisher got my attention and said, "Ed, I want you to meet an amazing young author." He introduced me to her, and I asked her about her book. After a few moments, she noticed my book, *The Difference a Father Makes*, and asked me, "Did you write this book?" To which I proudly said, "Yes, I did." She looked me in the eye and said, "Thanks a hell of a lot!" Puzzled by her statement, I asked her to explain.

"My dad is a pastor who came to your conference, bought this book, and read it. He then bought a ring as you did for your daughter and took me out on a date to bless me to be a woman. It had been a time long since my dad had spent time with me. I was curious why he was taking me out to such a nice restaurant. At the end of the dinner, he got out of the booth and dropped to one knee. With a promise ring in his hand, he looked at me. I was shocked and interrupted him, saying, 'Dad, what the hell do you think you're doing? So you think you can just read Ed McGlasson's book and bless me? Do you think you can just give me a ring and call me to be a woman and that will fix our relationship? I don't even like you right now! And until I like you, I won't let you bless me.'" Her bitterness toward her dad kept her from receiving because she had not been able to forgive him for the hurt that she had received from him.

She contacted me a year later and told me that it took a lot of daddy date nights and long talks before forgiveness was asked for and given. She also said, "After I forgave my dad, I told him that I was ready to receive his blessing. I asked if he would take me out again, to give me a ring, and to bless me." She went on to tell me, "I wasn't able to accept the first blessing because my dad thought it was just magic and that he just needed to say the words to heal our relationship. But what my dad needed to do was to have my heart first."

A blessing cannot be transferred to the ones we love without forgiveness. So how do you learn how to forgive and receive forgiveness?

Learning to Forgive

I had to learn how to receive God's forgiveness for myself before I could ask for forgiveness from my kids. Many of us have been brought up by parents who treated us harshly for not following the rules. The combination of imperfect parents and imperfect kids with harsh enforcement of the rules usually results in wounds and resentment in the children. Learning that our heavenly Father is not harsh and demanding but rather is full of mercy and forgiveness is the first step in building a culture of forgiveness in our families.

> "But the wisdom from above is first pure, then peaceable, gentle, reasonable, full of mercy and good fruits, unwavering, without hypocrisy." (James 3:17, NASB)

If our parenting style includes some harshness, it suggests that we haven't fully received the Father's blessing of mercy and forgiveness for ourselves; we haven't received "the wisdom from above." If we haven't received God's mercy and forgiveness, we won't have the mercy to give to our family when irritated, offended, or hurt. We can't pour forgiveness from a cup of harshness.

The second step is learning to offer the same generous amount of forgiveness to our family that the Father offers us. In my early days of fathering, I was quite impatient with my wife and kids if they didn't follow my direction. I had to learn how to forgive their small irritations before I could learn to be patient with them. As I began to appreciate how God had forgiven me for so many mistakes,

He filled me with a desire to offer the same generous forgiveness I had received. As my practice of forgiveness expanded, so too did my patience.

The third step, asking for forgiveness, was possible once I had set the example of forgiveness. As forgiveness became a way of life for us, the bitterness caused by my harsh-coach fathering style began to disappear. When I began to hear my children work through their problems with one another by forgiving each other, I saw how powerful it was for me as a father to model forgiveness to my kids. Forgiveness helped me win back the hearts of my wife and children.

Bitterness is pandemic today. Families break up because of bitterness. Children remain bitter regarding how they were treated by their parents, sometimes for a lifetime. As a result, they don't learn how to have healthy relationships with their loved ones. Husbands and wives become resentful of one another because of bitterness. Every family needs a culture of forgiveness to replace bitterness.

> "Let all bitterness and wrath and anger and clamor and slander be put away from you along with all malice. Be kind to one another, tender-hearted, forgiving each other, just as God in Christ also has forgiven you." (Eph. 4:31-32)

When Adam sinned, he not only brought sin into the world, but his sin also brought bitterness. Adam's family became infected with bitterness, which is evidenced by the fact that Adam's son Cain killed his brother Abel because he was bitterly angry with him. The lack of forgiveness and the bitterness inherited from Adam are still responsible for the breakdown of family relationships. With approximately half of all marriages ending in divorce, the need for forgiveness to heal bitterness in our families is greater than it ever has been. What is God's answer to this bitterness pandemic?

> "For as by the one man's disobedience the many were made sinners, so by the one man's obedience the many will be made righteous." (Rom. 5:19)

Adam introduced death along with bitterness through His sin, but Jesus offered life and relief from bitterness through the blessing of His sacrifice, which provided us forgiveness for our sins. Therefore, once we receive Jesus' mercy and forgiveness for our sins, how can we refuse to forgive and remain bitter toward those who hurt us? Jesus offered forgiveness to us while we were completely spiritually dead in our sin. He didn't wait until we made things right with God to offer forgiveness.

> "But God, being rich in mercy, because of the great love with which he loved us, even when we were dead in our trespasses, made us alive together with Christ—by grace you have been saved." (Eph. 2:4–5)

When we learn how to receive forgiveness for ourselves, it changes our heart in the way we forgive others. And when we learn to model what forgiveness looks like and ask for forgiveness, it changes our family's hearts. When we learn to forgive in the same way God forgives us, we have given the greatest gift in a world that has gone into the abyss of bitterness: the power of forgiveness.

It is not a journey for the faint of heart. But, winning back the hearts of my family was the beautiful transfer of God's grace onto our relationships—as I continued becoming who God was calling me to be: the husband and father my family needed.

Is Jesus' Blood Enough?

Have you ever had people hurt you whom you didn't want to forgive? I have met too many fathers, sons or daughters who have not spoken to one another for years. These are people who feel that the hurt they experienced is unforgivable. I have heard many of them say, "I can't forgive what they have done to me!"

I remember in my early days of learning about forgiveness that there were some people I forgave and then other people I dismissed. The people I dismissed were the people who had crossed a line in offending me. You know the line, the line where you say, "What you have just done to me I'm not going to forgive." Often we don't even think about not forgiving. We just hold back our love and become cold and distant to that person.

I had some people who hurt me as a pastor and they got put on that list. You know the list. Some of us have a list of those we see in public and walk the other way. We put on the Christian nice smile but we are not interested in having a relationship with them. That's not the way Jesus has forgiven us.

I remember someone who had hurt me and the Lord asked me a question in that small inside voice: "When I died on the cross, did I die for them too?" I said, "Of course You did, Lord." The Lord asked another question; "Was My blood enough to cover their hurt against you?" His question exposed that place in my heart where I had judged that person, where my emotions were in the prison of unforgiveness and bitterness. I said, "Of course Your blood is enough, Jesus." I realized in that moment that I was unwilling to fully accept the perfect work of Jesus on the cross because of my anger and bitterness. Something opened inside of my heart that day. I was set free from separating myself from people because of my unforgiveness and bitterness.

One of the greatest gifts that we can give somebody is the same mercy that God has given to us. When we extend mercy to somebody who doesn't deserve it, we are beginning to understand the power of forgiveness. True forgiveness happens when you're able to forgive people the same way Jesus has forgiven us. I am so glad that Jesus didn't cut me off from His mercy because I was lost and broken! How about you?

Connecting to My Father

"And rising very early in the morning, while it was still dark, he departed and went out to a desolate place, and there he prayed." (Mark 1:35)

Jesus did something very important every day. He connected to the voice and presence of His Father in prayer. The Bible says He rose early in the morning, all alone to hear from His Father. Jesus knew that to be able to hear and follow what the Father was doing was dependent on His connection to the Father every day. If Jesus needed time to connect with the Father every day, how much more do we need alone time in prayer with Him every day.

> "In that day you will ask nothing of me. Truly, truly, I say to you, whatever you ask of the Father in my name, he will give it to you. Until now you have asked nothing in my name. Ask, and you will receive, that your joy may be full." (John 16:23–24)

When do you meet with the Father in your schedule? Do you have a set time? I have learned something powerful about scheduling a regular time with the Father. When you set an appointment on your calendar with someone, what is your assumption about them? That they will show up for the appointment, right? When we set time in our calendar to meet with God and block out time to be with Him, we are assuming God is going to show up and meet with us. As simple as that sounds, it can have a profound effect on you as a man. We can say to our kids, "I am meeting with God this morning, to hear from Him, so that I can lead our family." Pray that God will open your mind to hear from Him and your heart to follow Him. It will change your life.

Praying and talking with the Father is a form of meditation—a time to quiet your mind from the everyday pressures of life to focus on what God has to say to you, like a son talking with his loving father. The Bible is God's Word. The combination of praying and reading God's Word will help you hear the Father's voice so that you can follow Him. Those moments of clarity and understanding, hearing a small voice inside your heart and mind, are the Father talking with you. To become the husband and father your family needs, spend time every day praying, reading God's Word, and talking with your heavenly Father.

Paul's words to the Ephesians are worth repeating in the context of talking with God:

"Blessed be the God and Father of our Lord Jesus Christ, who
has blessed us with every spiritual blessing in the heavenly places
in Christ, just as He chose us in Him before the foundation of
the world, that we would be holy and blameless before Him. In
love He predestined us to adoption as sons through Jesus Christ
to Himself, according to the kind intention of His will, to the
praise and glory of His grace, which he freely bestowed on us
in the Beloved." (Eph. 1:3-6)

When Edward was just about three years old, he came to my door during
one of my quiet times with God. I asked him, "What's up, son?"

He looked at me and asked, "What are you doing, Dad?"

I replied, "I'm spending time with God."

He paused for a minute, looked back at me, and asked, "Can I spend time
with you and God too?"

His question was amazing. I was discovering how my private life was affecting my son. He was watching me and learning to do what I was doing. Like every
son, they start out wanting to become just like their dad.

I invited him into my office and gave him one of my Bibles. He opened it
but it was upside down. He did not know that the Bible was upside down. There
were no pictures, like in his kids' Bible. He was watching me read the Bible, and I
started reading it quietly. I looked over at him mimicking me, moving his finger
across the page and moving his lips like he was reading the Word. I realized in
that moment that I was doing more to teach Edward about how to seek the Lord
than my best sermons ever did.

Do you see the access we have to the Father? The Creator of the universe is
our Father. He loves us! He will listen to us and answer our prayers. Jesus gave
us a promise about how our prayers are answered:

"In that day you will ask in my name, and I do not say to you
that I will ask the Father on your behalf; for the Father himself

loves you, because you have loved me and have believed that I came from God. I came from the Father and have come into the world, and now I am leaving the world and going to the Father." (John 16:26–28)

It is because the "Father Himself loves" us that we can go directly to Him and know that the Father loves to give good gifts to His children.

I remember when I was getting ready to quit my prayer session and the Father asked me a question: "What are you doing?"

I said, "Praying, Lord."

A few moments later He said, "Stop praying like a Christian."

I was puzzled. "What are You talking about? I thought I was supposed to pray like a Christian."

He asked me another question: "How did My Son, Jesus, pray?"

Then it hit me. He prayed like a Son. This moment completely changed my prayer life because I realized that God had given me complete access to Him as a son to a loving Father.

How do you pray?

The access we have to God through Jesus Christ opens the door for us to have a relationship with a Father who loves us and can't wait to answer our prayers. He can't wait to empower us to become the husbands and fathers that He wants us to be. He's not sitting in heaven disappointed about your life. He's sitting in heaven thinking about you and waiting for those moments of blessing that will turn you into the man, husband, and father your family needs.

He Will Dance over You

When my daughters were little, they used to come out into the atrium dancing and singing. My office has a sliding glass door that leads out to the atrium, so I had a front-row seat to these performances. When they would notice that I had stopped what I was doing and was watching them, they would run back and forth into their room, changing outfits and coming back to put on another performance.

I missed a lot of those moments as a young dad because I was so focused on myself and my job as a pastor. I look back now and see my girls just looking to catch my eye and my affection. They wanted to hear me say, "I love who God made you to be! You are so beautiful. Do you love to dance?" "Yes, Daddy! We love to dance! Watch me!" "I am watching! I love to watch you dance."

It reminds me of what the prophet Zephaniah wrote about God the Father:

> "He will take delight in you with gladness. With his love, he will
> calm all your fears. He will rejoice over you with joyful songs."
> (Zeph. 3:17, NLT)

I love this verse! I remember the first time I really understood it. I was watching my son Edward's scores come in online for a golf tournament he was in. He was playing well and was in position to win the tournament. I started blessing my son out loud in my office. I was so overcome by how much I loved him that just saying the words out loud didn't feel like enough, so I started singing and—believe it or not—I started dancing and twirling around in my office. I must have been making more commotion than I realized, because a few minutes later, my assistant burst into my office door to find me dancing, singing, and weeping over my son Edward. We both made eye contact and started laughing. I guess my attempt at dancing was shaking our whole building!

"He will rejoice over you with joyful songs" (Zeph. 3:17b). The Hebrew word here translated as "rejoice" means "dance, skip, leap, and spin around in joy." God's love is so intense that sometimes words are not enough—He has to dance with shouts of joy over us!

After my assistant left, I sat down at my desk, still filled with so much joy. In that moment, the Father spoke to me with that inside voice: "Ed, you should hear the song I am singing over you right now!"

Beloved, He is singing and dancing over you right now! Can you hear Him?

Personal Insights

1. Do you use advice and direction more than questions when talking with your wife and children?

2. Have you wounded your family with your harshness?

3. Are you building a culture of forgiveness in your family?

4. Are you receiving like Jesus did by regularly connecting to the Father and talking to Him as a son?

Key Takeaways

Hearing the Father's voice. It isn't until we hear God the Father's voice for ourselves, through Christ, that our hearts start changing from being a coach, belting out instructions and to-do lists, to being a loving, present father. I believe that every father wants to be that kind of dad. We love our children, and we want to make the most significant difference possible in their lives so that they can become everything that God has created them to be.

Why questions? Jesus was always asking His disciples questions. Jesus didn't rule over His disciples like a typical leader of the day. He discipled them like a loving Father so that they could learn like a son. He didn't try to overpower them with His authority to protect them from mistakes; He asked questions to help them learn how to hear from God the Father themselves. Questions are a powerful way for you to discern what the Father is doing in the lives of those whom you love.

Forgiveness. One of the greatest gifts that we can give somebody is the same mercy that God has given to us. When we extend mercy to somebody who doesn't deserve it, we are beginning to understand the power of forgiveness. True forgiveness happens when we're able to forgive people the same way Jesus has forgiven us. I had to learn how to receive God's forgiveness for myself before I could ask for forgiveness from my kids. If we haven't received God's mercy and forgiveness, we won't have the mercy to give to our family when irritated, offended, or hurt. We can't pour forgiveness from a cup of harshness.

Connecting with the Father. Jesus did something very important every day. He connected to the voice and presence of His Father in prayer. The Bible says that He rose early in the morning, all alone, to hear from His Father. Jesus knew that to be able to hear and follow what the Father was doing was dependent on His connection to the Father every day. If Jesus needed time to connect with the Father every day, how much more do we need alone time in prayer with Him every day?

> "And rising very early in the morning, while it was still dark, he departed and went out to a desolate place, and there he prayed."
> (Mark 1:35)

How To's

1. How do you build your life around receiving like Jesus did and being fathered by God?

What would it mean to you to have uninterrupted time with the Father every day? To know Him as a Father has been an amazing part of my story and it will be for you too. There are four parts of my time each day with the Father.

First, I find a place and give my first moments to worship. My goal is to connect and recenter my heart in the middle of the perfect love of the Father, His Son, Jesus, and the Holy Spirit. With that group surrounding me, nothing will be impossible.

Second, I open my Bible, read like a son, and listen to His voice. When God speaks something to you, write it down, including the date; highlight the text and write a note in the margin. If you fill your heart with His words, you will train your heart and mind to hear Him speaking to you.

Third, I write down my prayers, the things I learn, my questions, and the words He speaks into me in a journal. It can be a paper journal or electronic. Make it yours, and carry it with you everywhere you go, because you never know when He is going to speak to you. As I wrote in an earlier chapter, all of my books and sermons have come from my time with the Father.

Fourth, I carry my prayer list with me and pray out loud for the things that I need from my Father in heaven. I learned from Coach Bill Macartney, the founder of Promise Keepers, that "our next breakthrough is a prayer away. You can change your family history more on your knees than anything else you do."

2.   How do you begin to heal the hurt and reconnect with your kids?

Many of us have hurt our kids without even knowing it. I have learned that if you don't have the hearts of your kids, they won't listen to your advice, no matter how good it is. Learning to ask great questions will help you reconnect with your kids. Here is a great first question that has helped me reconnect with my kids: "Can you help me understand if there are some things I have done that have hurt you so that I can ask for forgiveness?"

Your goal here, Dad, is to ask questions to understand the hurt so that you can ask for forgiveness. This question has opened the door with my children in profound ways and has taught me to humble myself so that I can reconcile with them. It will teach your kids what forgiveness looks like. Don't get discouraged if they don't immediately respond. Keep asking until they forgive you! Don't give up. You are teaching your family how to forgive one another. It is one of the most powerful things a father can do!

One day you will witness your kids asking forgiveness from their future spouses and your grandkids, and you will remember those first moments when you modeled forgiveness and the healing began. I have, and so will you!

Send me an email on how can we pray for you and your kids?
edtandy@blessingofthefather.com

3.   How do you begin to heal the hurt and reconnect with your wife?

Your wife's heart is just like your kids' hearts. If you don't have it, you will know it, and your relationship will not grow. How many of you had dads who modeled and taught you how to love and lay down your life for your wife? Probably not many of you. Here are three steps for healing the hurt and reconnecting with your wife.

First, ask her, "Are there some things I have done that have hurt you so that I can ask for forgiveness?" It is okay if you are shaking when you ask this. It really does take a lot of courage to ask your wife this question—to listen, understand, and ask her to forgive you. Be specific: "Will you forgive me for …?" (Ladies, if you are reading these words because you are buying this book for your man, be gentle with him. Most men have never had a dad show them how to do this.)

Second, be intentional about building ways to reconnect with your wife. Schedule a regular weekly date night, and write down all of your important anniversaries in your calendar. Ask her about the things she loves doing and do them with her.

My wife told me a couple of years ago that she wanted to go ballroom dancing, and yes, yours truly got out there on the dance floor trying to bust a move; my wife could not stop laughing. Ask the Lord to help you make your marriage about her, and He will!

Send me an email on how can we pray for you and your wife?
edtandy@blessingofthefather.com

Prayer

Father, thank You for being my Father. Thank You for sending Your Son to lead me home to You. Thank You for transforming my life to look more like You and Your Son. I ask that You keep me focused on receiving from You and Your Holy Spirit every day. Help me win back the hearts of my wife and kids by modeling Your love, forgiveness, mercy, and generosity to them. Give me the same "like Father, like son," generous inside and out, true from start to finish life so that I can be the man, husband, and father You have made me to be. In Jesus' name, amen!

FROM THE AUTHOR

Ladies, are you looking for a great gift to help the men in your life?

"Without question, every father, son, brother, grandfather, and man should read this book!! The message is profound, deeply touching, and one of the most penetrating and important books of our time. The unparalleled message of the Father's blessing is one that cannot be silenced; our lives depend on it. If you love the men in your life, you will put this book in their hands."

Debbie Rasa

Order a copy at:
https://www.blessingofthefather.com/howtobecome

Would you like to receive the blessing of the Father every day?

We provide a free daily devotional by email to help you hear from God the Father who loves you.

"I wanted you to know how much I am enjoying your devotional. God has given you a gift to share with all of us! And you are opening the eyes of my heart to receive more of our Father's love! Thank you!!!"

D. Jasperson

Sign up at:
https://www.blessingofthefather.com/free-devotion

Would you like to attend one of our live events to learn more about how to become the husband and father your family needs?

"I can see the transformation occurring in my daughter, Haley's, life since the church service Sunday morning. She bought a dozen of your Difference a Father Makes books and she's been giving them out to friends in college. We've been having lunches and communicating again for the first time in years. This can only be of God's hands. Thank you for coming and sharing this life-altering message."

N. Smith

Register at:
https://www.blessingofthefather.com/mens-events/attend

Would you like to bring one of our live events to your church?

"We brought in Ed to do a men's event and it was off the charts great. From the youngest believer to the seasoned saint, the men were challenged, blessed, and empowered. One attendee was the former men's ministry Pastor at Willow Creek and he said it was the best men's retreat he had been on. If there is someone with a more powerful life message on the Father's blessing, the indwelling Christ, and straight-up zeal for the lost/evangelistic gifting in our movement, please send me their contact information ASAP! My catholic brother-in-law has not stopped thanking me for getting him out to hear Ed, he has been buying Ed's books to distribute to several Catholic priests that he knows. My only regret is we didn't get Ed in here sooner!"

Pastor T. Severson

Sign up at:
https://www.blessingofthefather.com/mens-events/schedule

Please help us transform another man into the husband and father his family needs by donating to our ministry.

"I am a father of two daughters and one son, ages 9, 5 and 10 months respectively. I struggle every day to be the man that God wants me to be and the father I know my children need. My grandmother gave me your book as a gift and I couldn't believe the tears that welled up inside me after I read the first few pages. I guess the whole reason I'm writing to say 'thank you' for writing a book that keeps me motivated and helps me better understand my role."

Michael S.

Donate at:
https://www.blessingofthefather.com/donate

Share your story about how the love and blessing of the Father has changed you!

"I just wanted to take time to thank you for the message you delivered at the retreat last weekend. I coach football and have witnessed the broken-ness in our players especially the scars left by the boy's fathers. The Lord put me at that retreat and you spoke right to my heart so I could receive the blessing of the Father for myself and learn how to father the young men I have the privilege to coach. I pray daily to be put in contact with 'orphans' and look forward to working in the mission field to rid the world of orphans."

Arnie P.

Write us an email today:
edtandy@blessingofthefather.com

Would you like to help transform another man by sending him a copy of this book?

"Ed, this is the book I wish I'd had to read one day before my son was born."

Bobb Biehl

"Christian since I was born. Now I'm His beloved son. Thanks for that amazing book. Greetings from Colombia, Pastor Ed."

Santiago M..

"'Ntate ED' (This is 'Father ED' in Sesotho one of the native languages in South Africa), thank you for the book. I prayed the prayer you lead me through in the book with all my heart. I have given my heart to Jesus Christ when I was in grade 9, but I've lived my life without knowing Him, without knowing the Father as my personal Dad. But I knew Him as a Father who was hard, ready to love me when I was only good enough and following his laws and commandments. I have tried my best to follow him, but have never known His love until yesterday. As I was reading the book, His love overwhelmed me, I dropped the book down and I started to sing, my heart was just overjoyed. To know that I have a Father who loves me oh so much. WOW. Thank you 'Ntate Ed!'"

Palesa

Send a Book at:
https://www.blessingofthefather.com/howtobecome

Made in United States
North Haven, CT
16 December 2022

29360944R00111